WILLIAMS-SONOMA

Casual Entertaining

The Best of Williams-Sonoma Lifestyles Series

Casual Entertaining

GENERAL EDITOR
CHUCK WILLIAMS

RECIPE PHOTOGRAPHY
RICHARD ESKITE

Contents

Introduction

For many people, there is something intimidating about the word "entertaining." The idea is appealing—a gathering of family or friends at home to enjoy your food and one another's company—but putting it into action can be stressful and time-consuming. You must plan, create the menu, do the shopping, clean the house, cook for hours, and, of course, play the host.

It is time to set such concerns aside. Entertaining is essentially about sharing good food and drinks with friends and family, and whether you are hosting a casual brunch or a festive dinner party, the experience can be fun and easy. Perhaps the first thing to do is to exchange the work "entertaining" for a less-intimidating, and thus less-stress-prompting, phrase: "having people over." Entertaining is not about being perfect. It is about creating and sharing a happy occasion that reflects who you are. More important, however, is that you have fun doing it, and do not try to outdo yourself. All you need are a few trustworthy recipes, including some that lend themselves to being made ahead of time, and you are already off to a great start. Included in this book are scores of recipes that minimize last-minute pressure in the kitchen and maximize flavor at the table, and thus are guaranteed to create the ideal mood for any occasion.

Casual entertaining is about creating a mood of relaxation and comfort that is carried through every aspect of the party. Even the most informal party can be the most gracious occasion and cause for celebration. If you work during the week, Saturday is the perfect time to entertain, because it gives you a chance to really prepare and get ready, working in shopping time and chalking off ingredient prep and make-ahead dishes during your free time as the weekend approaches. On the day of the party, you can exercise your culinary expertise with more challenging dishes, or put extra time into a homemade dessert. But weeknight entertaining has plenty of advantages for bringing people together; just keep things casual, with simple main courses and store-bought desserts.

Once you remove the stress of entertaining, you are able to put both yourself and your guests at ease. The easy-to-make recipes in this book are about making the evening relaxing and enjoyable. Orecchiette with Broccoli and Pine Nuts (page 93) is perfect for a midweek neighborhood gathering, while the Pan-Seared Halibut with Baby Vegetables (page 110) is an impressive crowd pleaser for a Saturday night dinner party. Enjoy Texas-Style Chili (page 173) while watching the game on a chilly Sunday afternoon. For complete menu ideas, turn to pages 12–13.

ENTERTAINING WITH FRIENDS AND FAMILY

Having friends visit for the weekend is one of the most enjoyable ways to entertain. It offers a chance to catch up on old times and to make new memories, often while gathered around the table for a meal. This book includes a chapter on brunch entertaining to guide you through a weekend with friends. But too many weekend hosts forget one essential ingredient for success, which is to make the experience as pleasurable for themselves as it is for their guests. They try to do too much, to make too grand of an impression, and often end up spending more time at the stove than with their friends. But for any entertaining, from leisurely to short and simple, it is important to learn tricks and techniques and to adopt an overall approach that allow you to spend less time in the kitchen and more time enjoying yourself.

One sensible strategy is to solicit your guests' help in the kitchen. This and many other suggestions throughout the book help make entertaining smooth, including tips for welcoming friends; suggestions for menu planning, and stocking the pantry; and ample inspiration for making every meal memorable. The goal is a simple one: to make both you and your guests look forward to the next invitation.

PLANNING A PARTY

The first and most obvious thing to focus on when entertaining is selecting a menu. To do this well, pay attention to the seasons and create a menu with a variety of dishes that take varying levels of effort.

Once you have an idea about what you will serve, think about *how* you will serve the meal. Remember that simplicity is a style that never fails. The more you plan ahead of time, the less you will have to worry about at the last minute. For groups of 8 or more, buffets are your best choice. Plan to arrange the food in the order that it will be eaten. For smaller groups, serve food family-style from passed platters and bowls.

Setting up a bar or beverage tray in advance will make the evening with friends run more smoothly—even an intimate gathering. Once you have your menu in mind, call your local wine store or a wine-savvy friend and ask for recommendations. Seeking advice is a great way to take more pressure off the host, although in the end, deciding which wines or special drinks will work best with a meal is largely a matter of personal taste, and affords the host another opportunity to put his or her own touch on the event.

A good host keeps everyone happy without anyone noticing. And the key to being that kind of host is to keep things uncomplicated and organized for yourself. Do as much as you can ahead of time, and let prepared foods and quality ingredients take you the rest of the way. Remember, your attitude is important: If you're relaxed and having fun, your guests will be, too. Don't worry about trying to impress anyone—keep in mind your guests simply want to spend a few memorable hours with you sharing a meal. Use the menus in this book (pages 12–13) for inspiration and feel free to mix and match, if you like, to find what works best for you. You'll discover that no matter what you make or how you serve it, if you make the process easy, you will find that entertaining as one of life's joys.

All the recipes here were chosen to inspire and reflect a relaxed yet vibrant mood in their presentation—and what they celebrate is friendship. There is no thought of impressing guests with fancy food or of fussing over elaborate decorations. The dishes and drinks satisfy without stealing the show. The guests will feel as if they are family, the host will get to join the party, and the laughter and lively conversation will flow naturally as the hours slip by. Of course, entertaining cannot always be a spur-of-the-moment affair, but you can approach any entertaining occasion, even a formal dinner party planned weeks in advance, with that same spirit of informality, spontaneity, and casual ease.

Menu Planning

The recipes in this book were developed to complement one another, resulting in scores of different menus for both small and large parties. The eight examples here represent only a handful of the many possible combinations. Feel free to use any or all of the recipes on any given occasion.

Italian Lunch al Fresco

Fava Bean and Pecorino Salad

Pizza with Tomatoes, Olives, and Pancetta

Angel Hair Pasta with Spring Vegetables

Pink Grapefruit Granita

Weekend Dinner Party

Crisp Vegetable Crêpes

Beef Braised in Star Anise Sauce

Steamed White Rice

Pear Tart with Walnuts

Open House*

Garlic-Rubbed Baguette with Chicken, Tomatoes, and Ta;penade

Spring Wrap of Wild Asparagus, Teleme Cheese, and Chervil

Carrot, Apple, and Red Cabbage Salw with Ginger Vinaigrette

Lime-Pecan Butter Cookies

*All items can be served at room temperature

Pan-Asian Dinner

Hot-and-Sour Vegetable Soup

*Chicken and Asparagus
with Spicy Black Bean Sauce*

Pad Thai

Coconut-Banana Pancake Rolls

Weekend Brunch

Bloody Mary

Old-Fashioned Pecan Sticky Buns

Ham and Cheddar Cheese Gratin

*Red, White and
Blueberry Fruit Bowl*

Sunday Supper

Purchased Corn Bread

Fried Chicken with Herbs

Spicy Macaroni and Cheese

Poached Pears and Blueberries

Seaside Dinner

Warm Shrimp Salad with Salsa Verde

*Pan-Seared Halibut with
Baby Vegetables*

Lemon-Almond Butter Cake

Casual Summer Supper

*White Bean Salad with Red, Green
and Yellow Peppers*

Chicken, Sausage, and Seafood Paella

Mixed Berry Shortcakes

Romantic Dinner
for Two

*Spring Lettuces with Grapefruit
and Sautéed Scallops*

Veal Piccata

Chocolate Mousse

Champagne

Starters & Small Plates

Crisp Vegetable Crepes

1¼ cups (6½ oz/200 g) rice flour

1 teaspoon turmeric

½ teaspoon sugar

½ teaspoon salt

1 cup (8 fl oz/250 ml) unsweetened coconut milk

½ lb (250 g) skinless, boneless chicken breast halves

½ lb (250 g) medium shrimp (prawns)

6 cloves garlic

6 shallots

5 medium carrots

1 red bell pepper (capsicum)

2 yellow summer squashes

1½–2 lb (750 g–1 kg) mung bean sprouts

2 cups (4 oz/125 g) small broccoli florets

½ cup (½ oz/15 g) *each* fresh cilantro (coriander) and mint leaves

¼ cup (¼ oz/7 g) loosely packed fresh Thai or sweet basil leaves

6 tablespoons (3 fl oz/90 ml) peanut or vegetable oil

Salt and freshly ground pepper

In a bowl, combine the rice flour, turmeric, sugar, and salt. Add the coconut milk and 1 cup (8 fl oz/250 ml) water and stir to blend thoroughly to make a batter. Cover and refrigerate the batter until ready to cook.

Cut the chicken crosswise into thin strips. Shell and devein the shrimp, then halve lengthwise and pat dry. Next, prepare the vegetables: mince the garlic; thinly slice the shallots; peel and shred the carrots; seed and finely julienne the bell pepper; and julienne the summer squashes. Set the ingredients each in separate bowls near the stove along with the bean sprouts, broccoli, cilantro, mint, and basil, also in separate bowls.

Heat a nonstick wok or nonstick 9-inch (23-cm) frying pan over medium-high heat. Add 1 tablespoon of the oil, one-sixth of the garlic, and one-sixth of the shallots and toss and stir until golden brown, about 1 minute. Add one-sixth each of the chicken and shrimp and toss and stir until the chicken is opaque, about 2 minutes. Season with salt and pepper to taste. Spread the chicken mixture on the pan bottom.

Stir the batter until smooth. If it is too thick, adjust with water, 1 tablespoon at a time until it is the consistency of heavy cream. Pour ⅓ cup (3 fl oz/80 ml) into the pan and tilt the pan to spread the batter evenly over the pan bottom and up the sides. Scatter one-sixth each of the carrots, bell pepper, squashes, bean sprouts, and broccoli in the center. Cover, reduce the heat to medium, and cook until steam seeps out from under the lid, about 4 minutes. Uncover, raise the heat to medium-high, and cook until the crêpe shrinks away from the pan sides, about 2 minutes longer. Scatter one-sixth each of the cilantro, mint, and basil over the vegetables. Using a spatula, lift the edge to check if the underside is crisp and brown, then fold the crepe like an omelet and slide onto a plate. Cut the crêpe crosswise into 4–6 pieces. Prepare the remaining crêpes.

Makes 6 crepes; serves 6

Focaccia with Gorgonzola, Pine Nuts, and Green Onions

To make the dough, in a bowl, using a wooden spoon, stir together the yeast, ¹/₄ cup (2 fl oz/60 ml) warm water (115°F/46°C), and ¹/₄ cup (1¹/₂ oz/45 g) of the flour. Let stand until foamy, about 20 minutes. Add the remaining 1³/₄ cups (8¹/₂ oz/270 g) flour, the salt, ²/₃ cup (5 fl oz/160 ml) cold water, and olive oil. Stir until the dough pulls away from the sides of the bowl. Turn out the dough onto a well-floured work surface and knead until soft, supple, and smooth yet still moist, 7–10 minutes. Place the dough in a clean, oiled bowl, turning it once to coat with the oil. Cover the bowl with plastic wrap, transfer to a warm place, and let the dough rise until doubled in bulk, 1–2 hours.

Meanwhile, make the topping: In a small, dry frying pan over medium heat, toast the pine nuts, stirring constantly, until golden, about 1 minute. Remove from the heat, pour into a bowl, and let cool. When cool, add the Gorgonzola, fontina, and green onions. Toss to mix well.

About 45 minutes before serving, place a pizza stone or baking tiles on the bottom rack of the oven and preheat to 500°F (260°C).

On a lightly floured work surface, punch down the dough and divide it in half. Shape each half into a smooth ball. Roll out 1 ball into a round 7 inches (18 cm) in diameter and ¹/₂ inch (12 mm) thick. Transfer the dough to a well-floured pizza peel or a rimless baking sheet. Scatter half of the cheese mixture evenly over the surface to within ¹/₂ inch (12 mm) of the edge.

Slide the dough round onto the heated stone or tiles and bake until golden and crisp, 10–12 minutes. Carefully slip the peel or baking sheet under the focaccia and transfer it to a cutting board. Repeat with the remaining dough and cheese mixture.

While the second round is baking, cut the first focaccia into 6 wedges and serve.

Makes two 7-inch (18-cm) rounds; serves 6

FOR THE DOUGH:

2 teaspoons active dry yeast

2 cups (10 oz/315 g) all-purpose (plain) flour or bread (hard-wheat) flour, plus flour for dusting

¹/₂ teaspoon salt

1 tablespoon extra-virgin olive oil

FOR THE TOPPING:

¹/₄ cup (1¹/₄ oz/37 g) pine nuts

¹/₄ lb (125 g) Gorgonzola cheese, at room temperature, crumbled

2 oz (60 g) fontina cheese, shredded

2 green (spring) onions, thinly sliced

Vegetable Samosas

These popular Indian-style turnovers are traditionally fashioned with hand-made flour-and-shortening dough. Puff pastry is an easy and equally delicious substitute. These crisp snacks can be made with your choice of vegetables in other seasons.

2 large russet potatoes, peeled and cut into 2-inch (5-cm) pieces

1 teaspoon curry powder

6 tablespoons (3 fl oz/90 ml) vegetable oil

1/2 cup (2 oz/60 g) chopped yellow onion

1 carrot, peeled and coarsely grated

1/2 cup (2 1/2 oz/75 g) shelled English peas

3 tablespoons minced fresh cilantro (fresh coriander)

Salt and freshly ground pepper

1 package (17 1/4 oz/537 g) frozen puff pastry, thawed

1 egg beaten with 1 tablespoon water

2 teaspoons caraway seeds

Place the potatoes in a saucepan with water to cover and bring to a boil over high heat. Cook until very tender, 20–25 minutes. Drain and transfer to a bowl. Using a fork, mash the potatoes well, mixing in the curry powder and 3 tablespoons of the oil at the same time. Set aside.

In a sauté pan over medium heat, warm the remaining 3 tablespoons oil. Add the onion and sauté until softened, 3–4 minutes. Add the carrot and sauté until the carrot has softened, 3–4 minutes longer. Stir the onion and carrot into the potatoes. Bring a small saucepan three-fourths full of water to a boil, add the peas, and blanch for 1 minute. Drain and add to the potato mixture along with the cilantro. Mix well and season to taste with salt and pepper. Set aside to cool.

On a work surface, roll out the puff pastry very thin. Using a scalloped biscuit cutter 3 inches (7.5 cm) in diameter, cut out rounds. Place about 1 teaspoon of the potato mixture in the center of each round. Brush the edges of the rounds with the egg-water mixture, fold in half, and press the edges together to seal.

Preheat the oven to 400°F (200°C). Line a large baking sheet with parchment (baking) paper. Place the filled turnovers on the prepared baking sheet and brush with the remaining egg-water mixture. Sprinkle the tops with the caraway seeds. Cover and chill for 30 minutes.

Bake the samosas until golden brown, 15–18 minutes. Serve hot.

Makes about 2 dozen samosas; serves 12

Sizzling Garlic Shrimp with Sherry

Serve these succulent shrimp piping hot with lots of crusty bread for sopping up the delicious juices. Pimenton is available at Spanish markets and specialty-food stores. This recipe also serves 6 as a starter.

3 tablespoons extra-virgin olive oil

6 cloves garlic, thinly sliced

Pinch of red pepper flakes

1¼ lb (625 g) shrimp (prawns), peeled and deveined

½ teaspoon pimenton (optional)

⅓ cup (3 fl oz/80 ml) dry sherry

Salt and freshly ground black pepper

1½ teaspoons chopped fresh flat-leaf (Italian) parsley

In a large frying pan over medium-high heat, warm the olive oil. Add the garlic and red pepper flakes and cook, stirring, for 15 seconds. Add the shrimp and pimenton, if using, and cook, stirring, until the shrimp curl and turn bright pink, about 3 minutes. Add the sherry and continue to cook until the sherry is reduced by half, about 1 minute. Season to taste with salt and black pepper.

Transfer to a serving dish and garnish with the parsley. Serve at once.

Serves 2–4

Spring Wrap of Wild Asparagus, Teleme Cheese, and Chervil

In early spring, wild asparagus shoots start appearing. They are no larger than a pencil, very tender, and sweet. If wild spears are not available, choose cultivated asparagus of the same size.

Snap off the tough ends from the asparagus where they break naturally and discard. Place the spears in a steamer basket set in a saucepan over boiling water. Cover and steam until the asparagus is just barely tender when pierced with the tip of a sharp knife, about 2 minutes. Remove from the steamer and transfer to a plate.

In a frying pan over medium heat, warm the oil. When it is hot, lay 1 tortilla in the pan. Place 2 or 3 slices of cheese down the center of the tortilla and cook until the edges of the tortilla begin to curl and the cheese begins to melt, 2–3 minutes. Place 2 asparagus spears down the center on top of the cheese and sprinkle with 2 teaspoons of the chervil. Using tongs, transfer to a plate. Carefully roll up the tortilla to form a cylinder and place, seam side down, on a warmed platter or on warmed individual plates. Keep warm. Repeat until all the ingredients are used, adding more oil to the pan if necessary.

Serve the filled tortillas hot.

Serves 6

12 thin asparagus spears

1 teaspoon canola or other light vegetable oil, or as needed

6 flour tortillas, each 8 inches (20 cm) in diameter

3 oz (90 g) teleme cheese, thinly sliced

¼ cup (⅓ oz/10 g) chopped fresh chervil or fresh flat-leaf (Italian) Parsley

Albóndigas

Albóndigas, small meatballs made all over Spain, are among the most common tapas served both at bars and in homes. When made very small, they are added to soups, and when formed into larger balls, they can be served as a main course.

Preheat the oven 350°F (180°C).

To make the meatballs, in a bowl, combine the pork, veal, bread crumbs, garlic, parsley, coriander, salt, black pepper, cumin, and cayenne pepper. Mix well. Using clean hands, form the mixture into about 30 balls, each about 1 inch (2.5 cm) in diameter. As the individual balls are formed, place them on an ungreased baking sheet.

Bake the meatballs until almost firm to the touch, 10–12 minutes. Remove from the oven and set aside.

Meanwhile, make the sauce: In a frying pan over medium heat, warm the olive oil. Add the onion and garlic and cook, stirring occasionally, until soft, about 7 minutes. Add the tomatoes and wine and simmer slowly until thickened, about 15 minutes.

Add the meatballs, salt, and pepper to the sauce and continue to simmer slowly until the sauce thickens and the meatballs are cooked through, about 10 minutes.

Transfer the meatballs to a bowl and serve hot, warm, or at room temperature. Provide toothpicks for eating and a bowl to discard them.

Serves 6

FOR THE MEATBALLS:

3/4 lb (375 g) *each* ground (minced) pork and ground (minced) veal

1 cup (4 oz/125 g) fine dried bread crumbs

4 cloves garlic, minced

2 tablespoons chopped fresh flat-leaf (Italian) parsley

1 1/2 teaspoons ground coriander

3/4 teaspoon salt

1/2 teaspoon *each* freshly ground black pepper and ground cumin

Pinch of cayenne pepper

FOR THE SAUCE:

3 tablespoons olive oil

1 yellow onion, minced

2 cloves garlic, minced

3 cups (18 oz/560 g) peeled, seeded, and chopped (fresh or canned) tomatoes

1 cup (8 fl oz/250 ml) dry white wine

1/2 teaspoon *each* salt and freshly ground black pepper

Curried Butternut Squash Filo Squares

1 butternut squash, about
1 lb (500 g)

2 shallots, minced

3 tablespoons minced fresh
flat-leaf (Italian) parsley

1 tablespoon curry powder

Salt and freshly ground pepper

1/2 cup (4 oz/125 g) unsalted
butter

6 filo sheets, thawed in the
refrigerator if frozen

Preheat the oven to 375°F (190°C). Line a large baking sheet with parchment (baking) paper.

Cut the squash in half through the stem end and scoop out and discard the seeds and fibers. Place the squash halves, cut sides down, on the prepared baking sheet. Bake until softened, 20–25 minutes. Transfer the squash halves to a rack and let cool. Leave the oven on. Discard the parchment paper.

Scoop the flesh from the squash into a bowl and mash with a potato masher until smooth. Stir in the shallots, parsley, and curry powder. Season to taste with salt and pepper. Set aside.

Clarify the butter: Place the butter in a frying pan and melt over medium heat. Skim off the foam from the surface. Let the melted butter cool slightly, then pour off the clear yellow liquid into a clean pan; discard the white solids in the bottom.

Reline the baking sheet with parchment paper. Lay the stacked filo sheets on a cutting board and cut them lengthwise into quarters. Cover with a damp kitchen towel to keep them from drying out, removing only a few strips at a time as needed.

Lay 1 filo strip on a work surface. Top with a second strip. Put 1 tablespoon of the squash filling about 1/4 inch (6 mm) from one end and fold the strip over 3 or 4 times to form a square. It will be open on 2 sides. Brush a third strip of filo with the clarified butter and wrap it around the square over the open sides. Place the square on the prepared baking sheet. Brush lightly with butter. Repeat with the remaining filo strips and filling to make 8 squares.

Bake the squares until golden brown, 15–18 minutes. Transfer to a serving dish and serve immediately.

Makes 8 squares; serves 4

STARTERS & SMALL PLATES | 27

Bruschetta with Tomatoes and Basil

Bruschetta—thick slices of rustic bread grilled, rubbed with garlic and olive oil, and sprinkled with coarse salt—celebrates the olive harvest. Serve at the height of summer when tomatoes are at their prime.

6 slices coarse country bread, each about 1/3 inch (1 cm) thick

2 cloves garlic, halved lengthwise

1/4 cup (2 fl oz/60 ml) good-quality extra-virgin olive oil

12 thin tomato slices

Coarse salt

6 fresh basil leaves

Prepare a medium-hot fire in a charcoal grill or preheat the broiler (griller).

Place the bread slices on the grill rack 4–5 inches (10–13 cm) from the fire and grill, turning once, until golden on each side, 30–60 seconds. If using the broiler, place the bread slices 4–5 inches (10–13 cm) from the heat source and grill, turning once, until golden on each side, 30–60 seconds.

Transfer the bread to a work surface and, while still warm, rub the slices lightly on both sides with a garlic clove half, handling the toasted bread as if it were a grater. Place the olive oil in a small bowl and brush each bread slice on one side with some of the oil. Top each slice with 2 tomato slices. Sprinkle the tomato slices with coarse salt. Stack the basil leaves on top of one another, roll up lengthwise, and slice crosswise into thin ribbons. Garnish the tomatoes with the sliced basil.

Arrange the bruschetta on a platter and serve immediately.

Serves 6

Big Island Poke

Poke (pronounced "POE-kay") is a Hawaiian dish of marinated fish that is usually combined with seaweed. Arame, a dried, subtly flavored black seaweed found at most health-food stores can be used here.

In a bowl, combine the soy sauce, ginger, garlic, red pepper flakes, and 1 teaspoon of the sesame oil. Stir well, then divide the mixture evenly between 2 bowls. Add the tuna to 1 bowl and toss to coat well. Reserve the second bowl of soy sauce mixture. Cover the fish and let stand at room temperature for 20 minutes.

Heat a large nonstick frying pan over high heat. First, add the remaining 1 teaspoon sesame oil and olive oil and swirl to coat the pan evenly. Then, add the onion and bell pepper and toss and stir until softened, about 4 minutes. Finally, add the bok choy and snow peas and toss and stir until tender, about 2 minutes. Stir in the reserved soy sauce mixture and cook for 1 minute.

Push the vegetables to the far side of the pan and add the tuna and its marinade to the empty part of the pan. Toss and stir until the tuna is opaque but still pink in the center, about 2 minutes.

Remove the pan from the heat and transfer the tuna and vegetables to a warmed serving platter. Serve at once.

Serves 4

¼ cup (2 fl oz/60 ml) soy sauce

¼ cup (1¼ oz/37 g) peeled and minced fresh ginger

2 tablespoons minced garlic

½ teaspoon red pepper flakes

2 teaspoons Asian sesame oil

1 lb (500 g) ahi tuna fillet, cut into 1-inch (2.5-cm) cubes

1 tablespoon olive oil

1 small yellow onion, cut into 1-inch (2.5-cm) cubes

1 red bell pepper (capsicum), seeded and cut into 1-inch (2.5-cm) pieces

½ lb (250 g) baby bok choy, coarsely chopped

5 oz (155 g) snow peas (mangetouts), trimmed and halved on the diagonal

Saucisson en Croûte

1 garlic sausage, about 2 lb
(1 kg), 12 inches (30 cm) long

½ head garlic, unpeeled

2 cups (16 fl oz/500 ml)
dry red wine

FOR THE PASTRY CRUST:

3 cups (15 oz/470 g)
all-purpose (plain) flour

1 teaspoon dried *fines herbes*
(parsley, tarragon, chives)

½ teaspoon salt

1 cup (8 oz/250 g) chilled
unsalted butter, cut into
tablespoons

1 egg

1 egg beaten with 1 tablespoon
water for an egg wash

FOR THE MUSTARD SAUCE:

1 tablespoon firmly packed
golden brown sugar

2 teaspoons balsamic vinegar

1 teaspoon fresh lemon juice

½ cup (4 oz/125 g)
whole-grain Dijon mustard

⅓ cup (2½ oz/75 g) smooth
Dijon mustard

1 small clove garlic, minced
with a pinch of salt

Prick the sausage in 5 or 6 places and place in a large nonaluminum frying pan over high heat. Add the garlic, wine, and cold water to cover. Cover, bring to a boil, reduce the heat to low, uncover, and simmer until the sausage is cooked, about 45 minutes. Transfer to a baking sheet lined with paper towels. Set a second baking sheet on top and weight with food cans. Let cool completely. Wrap and refrigerate.

To make the crust, in a bowl, stir together the flour, herbs, and salt. Add the butter and, using a pastry blender, cut it in until the mixture resembles coarse meal. In a small bowl, using a fork, beat together the egg and 2 tablespoons of ice water. Make a well in the flour mixture. Add the egg mixture and 2 more tablespoons ice water. Using the fork, mix, adding more ice water as needed, until the mixture holds together. Pat the dough into a ball, wrap in plastic wrap, and refrigerate for 1 hour.

Line a baking sheet with parchment (baking) paper. On a lightly floured work surface, roll out the pastry into an 8-by-16-inch (20-by-40-cm) rectangle. Place the sausage in the center and trim the pastry to allow for covering the sausage with an overlap of about ½ inch (12 mm) on all sides. Lift the long sides, brush the edges with water, then wrap the sausage, pressing the seam to seal. Fold up the ends, brush the edges with water, then press to seal. Brush all the seams with the egg wash. Transfer the wrapped sausage to the prepared baking sheet. Brush the entire pastry with the egg wash and cut a couple of steam vents in the top. Refrigerate, uncovered, for 1 hour. Preheat the oven to 375°F (190°C). Bake the sausage until the pastry is golden, about 45 minutes. Check after 25 minutes; if the crust is browning too fast, reduce the heat to 350°F (180°C).

To make the mustard sauce, in a small bowl, whisk together the brown sugar, vinegar, and lemon juice. Whisk in the mustards and garlic. Transfer the sausage to a platter and cut into thick slices. Pass the mustard sauce at the table.

Serves 6

Pita Pockets with Pork, Red Onion, and Chutney Mayonnaise

Prepare these pita pockets when an informal lunch or supper is on your weekend schedule. For pork, buy an extra tenderloin and increase the marinade accordingly. Alternatively, use leftovers from another favorite pork recipe.

To make the chutney mayonnaise, in a nonreactive bowl, combine the mayonnaise, chutney, green onion, ginger, curry powder, and pepper to taste. Stir well to mix thoroughly. Cover and refrigerate if not using at once.

To assemble the sandwiches, cut each pita bread in half to create 2 half-moon pockets. Spread the inside of each pita half with a generous 1 1/2 tablespoons of the chutney mayonnaise. Divide the pork evenly among the pita halves, then add a few onion slices and some spinach to each.

Arrange the pita halves in a napkin-lined basket or on a platter and serve at once.

Serves 6

FOR THE CHUTNEY MAYONNAISE:

1 cup (8 fl oz/250 ml) mayonnaise

1/4 cup (2 1/2 oz/75 g) mango chutney

2 teaspoons finely chopped green (spring) onion, including the tender green tops

2 teaspoons peeled and grated fresh ginger

1/2 teaspoon curry powder

Freshly ground pepper

FOR THE SANDWICHES:

6 pita breads, each 6 inches (15 cm) in diameter

3/4 lb (375–500 g) cooked pork tenderloin, thinly sliced

1 red onion, thinly sliced

1 cup (1 1/2 oz/45 g) packed spinach leaves, preferably baby spinach

Quesadillas with Heirloom Tomatoes and Grilled Corn Salsa

For these quesadillas, use any heirloom tomato variety you can find. Of course, ordinary sun-ripened summer tomatoes will work fine as well. A salsa of grilled sweet corn spiked with chiles and cilantro provides the perfect finishing touch.

2 lb (1 kg) assorted heirloom or other tomatoes, coarsely chopped

1½ teaspoons salt

1 teaspoon freshly ground pepper

4 ears of white or yellow corn, or a mixture, husks removed

2 tablespoons canola or other light vegetable oil

1 large, ripe avocado, halved, pitted, peeled, and cut into ½-inch (12-mm) dice

½ cup (3 oz/90 g) minced red onion

¼ cup (⅓ oz/10 g) chopped fresh cilantro (fresh coriander)

1–2 serrano chiles, seeded and minced

2 cloves garlic, minced

2 tablespoons fresh lime juice

½ teaspoon chili powder

8 flour tortillas, each about 10 inches (25 cm) in diameter

½ lb (250 g) Monterey jack or other mild cheese, shredded

Prepare a medium-fire for direct-heat cooking in a charcoal grill. Place the grill rack 4–6 inches (10–15 cm) from the fire.

Place the chopped tomatoes in a bowl and add 1 teaspoon of the salt and ½ teaspoon of the pepper. Stir to mix and set aside.

Brush the ears of corn with 1 tablespoon of the oil. Place directly on the grill rack and grill, turning often, until tender and lightly bronzed, 8–10 minutes. Remove from the rack and let cool.

In a bowl, combine the avocado, onion, cilantro, chiles, garlic, lime juice, chili powder, and the remaining ½ teaspoon each of the salt and pepper. Cut off the kernels from the corn cobs and add them to the avocado mixture. Stir to mix well. Set aside.

In a frying pan over medium-high heat, heat the remaining 1 tablespoon oil. When it is hot, place 1 tortilla in the pan and cook until the edges begin to curl slightly, 1–2 minutes. Sprinkle one eighth of the cheese down the center of the tortilla. Using a spatula, fold the tortilla in half and press down on the top. Cook until the underside is golden brown, about 30 seconds, then turn and continue to cook on the second side until golden brown and the cheese has melted, about 30 seconds longer. Remove from the pan and keep warm. Repeat with the remaining tortillas.

Spoon several tablespoons of the tomatoes and the corn salsa inside each quesadilla and serve at once.

Serves 4

Seared Scallops with Tropical Salsa

A tropical-fruit and cucumber salsa provides a refreshing counterpoint to the richness of the sea scallops. Feel free to substitute any of your favorite fruits in the salsa. Take care not to overcook the scallops as they toughen quickly.

In a bowl, combine the pineapple, mango, cucumber, bell pepper, cilantro, lime juice, and chile to make a salsa. Toss well to mix. Season the salsa to taste with salt and pepper. Set aside.

In a large, nonstick frying pan over medium-high heat, warm the olive oil. Season the scallops with salt and pepper. Add half of the scallops to the pan and sear, turning once, until golden brown on both sides and opaque throughout, about 2 minutes on each side. Transfer the scallops to a warmed plate. Keep warm while cooking the remaining scallops in the same way.

Divide the scallops among warmed individual plates. Spoon the salsa over the top, dividing it evenly. Garnish with the lime slices and serve at once.

Serves 4

½ cup (3 oz/90 g) diced pineapple

½ cup (3 oz/90 g) diced mango

½ cup (2½ oz/75 g) diced cucumber

½ cup (2½ oz/75 g) diced red bell pepper (capsicum)

3 tablespoons chopped fresh cilantro (fresh coriander)

4 teaspoons fresh lime juice

1 jalapeño chile, seeded and minced

Salt and freshly ground pepper

2 tablespoons olive oil

16 sea scallops, about 1 lb (500 g) total weight, muscles removed

8 thin lime slices for garnish

Kettle-Seared Garlic-Pepper Mussels

This Vietnamese-style dish infuses fresh mussels with the intense flavors of garlic, pepper, and fish sauce. It is best made in a cast-iron kettle, helping the mussels to cook quickly. You can also use a Dutch oven.

2 tablespoons vegetable oil

6 large cloves garlic, chopped

2 large shallots, thinly sliced

1/2 teaspoon coarse sea salt or kosher salt

2–2 1/2 lb (1–1.25 kg) mussels, debearded and well scrubbed

2 tablespoons sugar

2 tablespoons fish sauce

1 teaspoon coarsely ground pepper

1 red jalapeño chile, seeded and finely diced

Fresh cilantro (fresh coriander) sprigs for garnish

Warm a 3-qt (3-l) cast-iron kettle or Dutch oven over medium-high heat. Add the oil, garlic, shallots, and salt and sauté until the garlic and shallots are golden brown, about 1 minute. Raise the heat to high and add the mussels, discarding any that do not close to the touch. Toss and stir to coat with the seasoned oil. Add the sugar, fish sauce, and pepper and stir to combine. Reduce the heat to medium-high, cover, and cook until the mussels open, 3–5 minutes. Using tongs, discard any mussels that failed to open.

The sauce should be the consistency of a light syrup. If the sauce is too thin, using a slotted spoon, transfer the mussels to a plate. Raise the heat to high and cook the sauce, stirring frequently, until reduced by one-third, 3–5 minutes. Return the mussels to the kettle or pot and toss to coat with the sauce.

To serve, transfer the mussels to a warmed large bowl or place the pot on a trivet on the table. Garnish with the chile and cilantro sprigs and serve at once.

Serves 4

Mussels with Feta and Tomatoes

This Mediterrenean-style dish can be made with other shellfish such as clams or shrimp (prawns). Serve with crusty bread to soak up the flavorful sauce left behind after eating the mollusks.

In a large frying pan over medium heat, warm the olive oil. Add the onion and cook, stirring occasionally, until soft, about 7 minutes. Raise the heat to high and add the tomatoes, wine, oregano, red pepper flakes, and vinegar. Stir well and bring to a boil. Reduce the heat to low and simmer uncovered, stirring occasionally, until thickened, 20–30 minutes.

Add the mussels to the pot, discarding any that do not close to the touch. Cover and cook until most of the mussels open, 2–3 minutes. Uncover and, using tongs, transfer the opened mussels to a bowl. Re-cover and continue to cook until all the mussels have opened, a minute or so longer. Transfer the additional opened mussels to the bowl and discard any that failed to open. Remove the pan from the heat.

When the mussels are just cool enough to handle, remove the meats from the shells and return them to the pan; discard the shells. Add the feta cheese to the pan and return the pan to medium heat. Bring to a gentle simmer and cook for until the mussels are heated through and the cheese is softened, about 30 seconds. Season to taste with salt and black pepper.

To serve, pour the mussels and their sauce onto a warmed platter and garnish with the parsley. Serve at once.

Serves 2–4

2 tablespoons olive oil

1 small yellow onion, minced

2 cups (12 oz/375 g) peeled, seeded, and chopped fresh tomatoes or canned

1 cup (8 fl oz/250 ml) dry white wine

1/4 teaspoon dried oregano

Pinch of red pepper flakes

1 teaspoon red wine vinegar

2 lb (1 kg) mussels, debearded and well scrubbed

6 oz (185 g) feta cheese, crumbled

Salt and freshly ground black pepper

1 tablespoon coarsely chopped fresh flat-leaf (Italian) parsley

Garlic-Rubbed Baguette with Chicken, Tomatoes, and Tapenade

Store-bought roasted chicken is put to good use in these sandwiches, which also call for prepared tapenade. Pack the sandwiches for an evening picnic at the beach or for lunch at an afternoon concert in the park.

1 baguette, 24 inches (60 cm) long and 2½ inches (6 cm) in diameter

3 tablespoons extra-virgin olive oil

1 large clove garlic, halved

¼ lb (125 g) creamy fresh goat cheese

About ¼ cup (2 oz/60 g) Tapenade (page 33) or purchased tapenade

1 roasted chicken, 2½–3 lb (1.25–1.5 kg), at room temperature, skin removed and meat sliced

2 or 3 plum (Roma) tomatoes, sliced

Leaves from 1 small bunch fresh basil

Freshly ground pepper

Place the baguette on a work surface and cut it on the diagonal into 4 equal pieces. Cut each piece in half horizontally. Brush the cut surfaces with the olive oil.

Place a stove-top grill pan over medium heat. When hot, place the bread, cut sides down, on the pan and grill until lightly browned, about 1 minute. Remove the bread from the pan and rub the cut surfaces with the cut sides of the garlic clove.

Spread the 4 bottom pieces of bread generously with the goat cheese, dividing it evenly. Smear a thin layer of the tapenade over the cheese. Layer the sliced chicken over the tapenade, and top with the tomato slices and several fresh basil leaves, again dividing the ingredients evenly. Sprinkle some fresh pepper over all.

Top the sandwiches with the bread tops and serve. Or, wrap each sandwich tightly in aluminum foil or plastic wrap and refrigerate until ready to serve.

Serves 4

Hero Sandwiches

These sandwiches are perfect to serve at a picnic when there is a bit of a chill in the air and you want to enjoy something substantial and satisfying. Accompany with a selection of mustards and other condiments so your guests can pick and choose.

Sprinkle the olive oil, vinegar, oregano, and Parmesan cheese over the cut surface of each roll half, dividing the ingredients evenly among the halves.

Arrange layers of the salami and mortadella over the bottom half of each roll, giving each an equal amount of each meat. If necessary, cut the meat slices to make sure that they fit the bread and are evenly divided among the sandwiches. Top with the Provolone cheese slices, again dividing equally.

Core the tomato and cut into 8 equal slices. Put 2 slices of tomato over the cheese on the bottom half of each roll. Arrange the lettuce strips on top and sprinkle 1 teaspoon of the pimiento over the lettuce on each roll.

Set the tops of the roll over the ingredients to make the sandwiches and serve at once. Or, wrap each sandwich tightly in aluminum foil or plastic wrap and refrigerate until ready to serve.

Serves 4

¼ cup (2 fl oz/60 ml) olive oil

1 tablespoon red wine vinegar

1 teaspoon dried oregano

2 tablespoons grated Parmesan cheese

4 crusty French or Italian rolls, each 5 to 6 inches long, halved hortizontally

¼ lb (125 g) thinly sliced salami, such as Genoa

¼ lb (125 g) thinly sliced mortadella or bologna

¼ lb (125 g) thinly sliced provolone cheese

1 large, firm tomato

½ head iceberg lettuce, cut into strips

4 teaspoons chopped pimiento

Crab Cakes with Avocado Salsa

Jalapeño and cayenne season these fabulous crab cakes served with an herb-laced avocado salsa. Only a small amount of bread crumbs is mixed into the crab cake mixture. Fresh bread crumbs are best, but you can use dried as well.

2 lb (1 kg) cooked lump crabmeat

1/2 cup (1 1/2 oz/45 g) minced green (spring) onions

1/2 cup (4 oz/125 g) minced pimiento

1/2 cup (4 fl oz/125 ml) mayonnaise

3 egg yolks, lightly beaten

1 tablespoon minced jalapeño chile, or to taste

1/2 teaspoon cayenne pepper

Salt and freshly ground black pepper

2 cups (4 oz/120 g) bread crumbs

1/3 cup (3 fl oz/80 ml) vegetable oil

FOR THE AVOCADO SALSA:

1 large Hass avocado

1 small red onion

1 tablespoon *each* chopped fresh tarragon and chervil

2 tablespoons fresh lime juice

1 teaspoon salt

Freshly ground black pepper

In a bowl, combine the crabmeat, green onions, pimiento, mayonnaise, egg yolks, jalapeño, cayenne pepper , and salt and black pepper to taste. Mix well. Add 1/2 cup (1 oz/30 g) of the bread crumbs and mix again. Fry about 1 tablespoon of the mixture in a little oil in a small sauté pan, then taste and adjust the seasonings.

Place the remaining 1 1/2 cups (3 oz/90 g) bread crumbs on a plate. Line a baking sheet with plastic wrap. Form the crab mixture into 8 cakes, each 1/2 inch (12 mm) thick. Coat each cake in the bread crumbs, place on the lined baking sheet, cover with plastic wrap, and chill in the refrigerator until firm, at least 3 hours or up to 6 hours.

Meanwhile, make the salsa: Halve, pit, and peel the avocado. Cut it into 1/4-inch (6-mm) dice and place in a bowl. Mince the onion and chop the tarragon and chervil and add them to the bowl with the avocado. Add the lime juice and stir the ingredients gently with a fork, then season with salt and pepper to taste. Cover with plastic wrap pressed directly onto the surface and refrigerate until serving.

Just before serving, in a large sauté pan over medium-high heat, warm the oil. Working in batches, add the crab cakes and sauté, turning once, until golden brown on both sides, about 4 minutes on each side. Transfer to paper towels to drain for about 2 minutes.

Serve on warmed individual plates. Pass the salsa at the table.

Serves 8

Salads & Soups

Squash and Coconut Milk Soup

Thai soups have a complex fusion of spicy, tangy flavors that taste refreshing and light. In this soup, chunks of winter squash add texture to broth enriched with coconut milk and seasoned with lemongrass, chiles, lime, and basil.

1 tablespoon dried baby shrimp (prawns)

4 shallots, quartered

2 red or green serrano or jalapeño chiles, seeded

1 stalk lemongrass, center white part only, chopped

2 1/2 cups (20 fl oz/625 ml) unsweetened coconut milk

2 cups (16 fl oz/500 ml) Chicken Stock (page 288) or broth

6 kaffir lime leaves

1 lb (500 g) kabocha, acorn, or butternut squash, peeled and cut into 3/4-inch (2-cm) pieces

1 tablespoon Thai fish sauce

1 tablespoon lime juice

1/2 teaspoon sugar

1/2 cup (1/2 oz/15 g) fresh basil leaves

Place the dried shrimp in a small bowl, add warm water to cover, and let soak until softened, about 10 minutes. Drain, reserving half of the liquid.

In a blender, combine the softened shrimp and reserved soaking liquid, shallots, chiles, and lemongrass. Process until a smooth paste forms.

Open the can of coconut milk without shaking it. Scrape the thick cream from the top into a large saucepan over medium-high heat. Stir in the shrimp-chile paste and bring to a boil. Reduce the heat to medium and cook, stirring occasionally, uncovered, until fragrant, about 5 minutes. Add the remaining coconut milk, the stock, kaffir lime leaves, and the squash and stir. Raise the heat to medium-high and bring to a boil. Reduce the heat to low and simmer, uncovered, stirring once or twice, until the squash is tender, about 15 minutes.

Just before serving, stir in the fish sauce, lime juice, sugar, and half of the basil leaves. Taste and adjust the seasonings. Ladle into bowls, garnish with the remaining basil leaves, and serve hot.

Serves 6

White Bean Salad with Red, Green, and Yellow Peppers

If you travel to Tuscany, you will find that Tuscans love cannellini beans. Cook them with garlic and Tuscany's golden olive oil and eat them warm, or make them into salads, such as this colorful antipasto, which is ideal for toting to a picnic lunch.

Pick over the beans and discard any misshapen beans or stones. Rinse the beans and drain. Place in a bowl, add plenty of cold water to cover, and let soak for 4 hours or up to overnight. Drain and place in a saucepan with water to cover by 4 inches (10 cm). Bring to a boil over high heat, reduce the heat to low, and simmer, uncovered, until the skins just begin to crack and the beans are tender, 30–40 minutes. Remove from the heat, drain, and transfer to a bowl.

In a small bowl, whisk together the olive oil and the 5 tablespoons (2$^{1}/_{2}$ fl oz/75 ml) vinegar to form a dressing. Season to taste with salt and pepper.

Add the dressing to the warm beans and let stand until the beans are cool, about 1 hour. Add the bell peppers, onion, garlic, and chopped oregano to the beans and mix well. Taste and add more salt, pepper, and vinegar, as needed. Serve at room temperature, garnished with the oregano sprigs.

Serves 6

1 cup (7 oz/220 g) dried cannellini beans

6 tablespoons (3 fl oz/90 ml) extra-virgin olive oil

5 tablespoons (2$^{1}/_{2}$ fl oz/ 75 ml) red wine vinegar, or as needed

Salt and freshly ground black pepper

1 red bell pepper (capsicum), seeded and cut into $^{1}/_{4}$-inch (6-mm) dice

1 green bell pepper (capsicum), seeded and cut into $^{1}/_{4}$-inch (6-mm) dice

1 yellow bell pepper (capsicum), seeded and cut into $^{1}/_{4}$-inch (6-mm) dice

1 small red onion, cut into $^{1}/_{4}$-inch (6-mm) dice

1 clove garlic, minced

1 tablespoon chopped fresh oregano, plus small sprigs for garnish

Panzanella

Here is an ingenious way to use up stale bread. The success of the recipe depends upon the type of bread you use. It must have a dense, coarse texture, rather than a light, cottony one. Full-flavored sun-ripened tomatoes are equally important to the final result.

½ lb (250 g) 2- to 3-day-old coarse country bread

6 ripe tomatoes, peeled, seeded, and coarsely diced

1 red onion, thinly sliced

1 English (hothouse) cucumber, peeled, seeded, and diced

2 tablespoons capers, rinsed

½ cup (½ oz/15 g) fresh basil leaves

2 tablespoons red wine vinegar

¼ cup (2 fl oz/60 ml) balsamic vinegar

¼ cup (2 fl oz/60 ml) extra-virgin olive oil

Salt and freshly ground pepper

Cut the bread into slices 1 inch (2.5 cm) thick. Place in a shallow bowl in a single layer and sprinkle with ½ cup (4 fl oz/125 ml) water. Let stand for 1 minute. Carefully squeeze the water from the bread. Tear the bread into rough 1-inch (2.5-cm) pieces and place on paper towels for 10 minutes to absorb the moisture.

In a bowl, combine the tomatoes, onion, cucumber, and capers. Tear the basil leaves into small pieces and add to the mixture. Add the bread pieces and toss carefully to avoid breaking up the bread too much.

In a small bowl, whisk together the red wine and balsamic vinegars and olive oil. Season to taste with salt and pepper. Drizzle over the bread-tomato mixture and toss gently to mix. Cover and refrigerate for 1 hour.

Transfer to individual bowls and serve immediately.

Serves 6

Spicy Asparagus Bean Salad with Garlic and Shallot Chips

In a small frying pan over medium-high heat, warm the 1 tablespoon oil. Add the chicken and sauté, breaking up any clumps, until opaque and crumbly, about 5 minutes. Transfer to a large bowl.

In a small, dry frying pan over medium heat, toast the coconut, stirring occasionally, until golden brown, about 5 minutes. Transfer to a plate and set aside.

Bring a saucepan three-fourths full of water to a boil. Add the beans and blanch until tender-crisp, about 1 minute. Drain and rinse under running cold water to stop the cooking. Cut into $^1/_4$-inch (6-mm) pieces. Add the toasted coconut, beans, shrimp, bell pepper, and the chiles to the chicken and stir to combine.

In a small 8$^1/_2$-inch (21.5-cm) frying pan over medium heat, warm the 2 cups (16 fl oz/500 ml) oil until the temperature reaches 325°F (165°C) on a deep-frying thermometer. Add the shallots and fry until golden brown and crisp, 5–8 minutes. Using a slotted spoon, transfer to paper towels to drain. Add the garlic to the heated oil and fry until golden brown and crisp, 5–8 minutes. Transfer to paper towels to drain.

To make the dressing, in a bowl, combine the lime juice, chile paste, fish sauce, and sugar. Whisk in 3 tablespoons of the coconut cream.

Pour the dressing over the salad, add the garlic and shallot chips, and toss gently to combine. Transfer to a platter. Drizzle with the remaining 1 tablespoon coconut cream and garnish with the peanuts. Serve immediately.

Serves 6

1 tablespoon vegetable oil, plus 2 cups (16 fl oz/500 ml) peanut or corn oil

6 oz (185 g) ground (minced) dark-meat chicken

3 tablespoons shredded unsweetened coconut

$^1/_2$ lb (250 g) asparagus beans or green beans, trimmed

$^1/_4$ lb (125 g) cooked shrimp (prawns), cut into $^1/_4$-inch (6-mm) pieces

$^1/_4$ red bell pepper (capsicum), cut into $^1/_4$-inch (6-mm) dice

2 serrano chiles, seeded and chopped

6 shallots, cut into thin slivers

8 cloves garlic, cut into thin slivers

FOR THE DRESSING:

$^1/_4$ cup (2 fl oz/60 ml) fresh lime juice

1 tablespoon Thai roasted chile paste

1 tablespoon Thai fish sauce

1 tablespoon sugar

4 tablespoons (2 fl oz/60 ml) coconut cream

3 tablespoons roasted peanuts, chopped

Green Papaya and Carrot Salad with Roasted Peanuts

The mild, tart flavor and crunchy texture of green papaya highlight this Vietnamese salad dressed with a spicy lime vinaigrette. Green papaya, a large immature cousin of the common papaya, is available whole and preshredded in Asian markets.

1½ lb (750 g) green papaya

1 carrot, peeled

FOR THE DRESSING:

1 small red chile, chopped

1 clove garlic, finely minced

1 tablespoon sugar

2 tablespoons Vietnamese fish sauce

1½ tablespoons lime juice with pulp

1½ tablespoons unseasoned rice vinegar

2 red jalapeño chiles, seeded and finely sliced

3 tablespoons chopped fresh cilantro (fresh coriander)

2 tablespoons chopped fresh Vietnamese mint

¼ cup (1 oz/30 g) chopped roasted peanuts, for garnish

Shrimp (prawn) chips, for serving

Cut the papaya in half lengthwise. Peel, then scrape out and discard the seeds. Using a mandoline fitted with the thin julienne slicing blade, shred the papaya into julienne strips no wider than ⅛ inch (3 mm). Shred the carrot into julienne strips. Place the shredded papaya and carrot in a bowl of ice water. Let stand until crisp, about 10 minutes.

Meanwhile, make the dressing: Place the red chile, garlic, and sugar in a mini food processor and process until a loose paste is formed. Alternatively, place the ingredients in a mortar and grind with a pestle. Transfer to a bowl and add the fish sauce, lime juice, and vinegar and stir to combine.

Drain the papaya and the carrot. Pat them dry and place in a large bowl. Add the jalapeño chiles, cilantro, and mint. Pour the dressing over the salad ingredients and toss to coat the ingredients evenly. Let stand for at least 10 minutes or up to 1 hour to absorb the flavors.

To serve, use tongs to pick up portions of the salad and shake gently to drain any excess liquid clinging to the salad. Arrange on individual bowls or plates, garnish with the peanuts, and accompany with the shrimp chips.

Serves 6

Carrot, Apple, and Red Cabbage Slaw with Ginger Vinaigrette

This colorful, crisp salad is an ideal accompaniment to Asian-inspired soups. Use chopped, dry-roasted peanuts instead of the sesame seeds, if you prefer. Julienned cooked beets can be used in place of the carrots.

FOR THE GINGER VINAIGRETTE:

1/2 cup (2 oz/60 g) peeled and sliced fresh ginger

1/4 cup (2 fl oz/60 ml) white wine vinegar

3/4 cup (6 fl oz/180 ml) peanut or canola oil

1 tablespoon sugar

1/2 teaspoon salt

1/2 teaspoon freshly ground pepper

1/4 cup (3/4 oz/20 g) sesame seeds

3 cups (9 oz/280 g) thinly sliced red cabbage

6 carrots, peeled and julienned

1 tart apple such as pippin or Granny Smith, halved, cored, and thinly sliced

To make the ginger vinaigrette, in a food processor or blender, combine the ginger and vinegar and purée until smooth. Transfer to a bowl and whisk in the oil, sugar, salt, and pepper. Set aside.

In a small dry frying pan over medium-high heat, toast the sesame seeds until they pop, about 5 minutes. Set aside.

In a bowl, combine the cabbage, carrots, and apple. Drizzle with the vinaigrette and toss to coat evenly. Top with the sesame seeds and serve at once.

Serves 6

Fava Bean and Pecorino Salad

Tender spring fava beans are prized in southern Italy, where they are enjoyed raw with pecorino cheese. Here, this pairing is turned into a delicate salad with the addition of lettuce, olive oil, and lemon juice.

First, shell the fava beans. Have ready a bowl of ice water. Bring a large saucepan three-fourths full of water to a boil. Add the favas and boil for 2 minutes, then drain. Immediately transfer to the bowl of ice water to stop the cooking, then drain.

Pinch off the ends and squeeze each bean free of its tough outer skin. If the beans are very small, they can be left unskinned.

In a bowl, mix together the beans, olive oil, and green onion. Season to taste with salt, pepper, and lemon juice. Tear the lettuce into bite-sized pieces and add to the bowl. Toss gently. Using a vegetable peeler, shave the pecorino cheese into paper-thin slices directly into the bowl. Toss gently. Taste the salad and adjust the seasonings. Serve at once.

Serves 4

4 lb (2 kg) fava (broad) beans

2¹⁄₂–3 tablespoons extra-virgin olive oil

2 tablespoons minced green (spring) onion, including the tender green tops

Salt and freshly ground pepper

Fresh lemon juice

8–12 soft lettuce leaves, preferably red

2 oz (60 g) young pecorino cheese

Three-Bean Salad with Toasted Coriander Vinaigrette

Three-bean salad is an old-fashioned summertime favorite. Here is an updated version that calls for fresh shelling beans, slender French snap beans, and pale wax beans. The flavor intensifies if the salad is allowed to marinate for at least 1 hour.

½ lb (250 g) fresh flageolet beans or other fresh shelling beans, shelled

1 lb (500 g) yellow wax beans, trimmed and cut into 2-inch (5-cm) lengths

1 lb (500 g) haricots verts, trimmed

1 teaspoon ground coriander

¼ cup (2 fl oz/60 ml) fresh lemon juice

2 tablespoons white wine vinegar

2 shallots, minced

¾ cup (6 fl oz/180 ml) safflower oil

1 teaspoon grated lemon zest

Salt and freshly ground pepper

Have ready a bowl of ice water. Bring a large saucepan three-fourths full of salted water to a boil. Add the shelling beans and boil until just tender, 10–15 minutes. Scoop the beans out of the water with a slotted spoon and immediately transfer to the ice water to stop the cooking. Scoop out of the ice water and set aside to drain. Repeat with the yellow wax beans and haricots verts, cooking the wax beans 7–8 minutes and the haricots verts about 5 minutes.

In a small, dry frying pan over medium heat, toast the coriander, shaking the pan occasionally, until aromatic, 2–3 minutes. Transfer to a plate to cool.

In a small bowl, combine the lemon juice, vinegar, and shallots. While whisking continuously, slowly drizzle in the safflower oil to form a vinaigrette. Stir in the lemon zest and toasted coriander, and season with salt and pepper to taste.

Combine all the beans in a large mixing bowl. Add the vinaigrette and toss to mix well. Let stand at room temperature for least 1 hour, or refrigerate for up to 3 hours. Serve at room temperature or chilled.

Serves 6–8

Hot-and-Sour Vegetable Soup

This Asian-inspired soup has a brisk spiciness that is wonderfully refreshing on a hot summer's day. Adjust the soup's heat to your personal taste by increasing or decreasing the number of chiles.

In a saucepan over medium heat, combine the coconut milk, stock, chiles, garlic, and lemongrass. Bring to a boil, then reduce the heat to medium-low. Simmer, uncovered, for 15 minutes to infuse the stock with the lemongrass and garlic.

Add the mushrooms and lime zest and cook until the mushrooms are tender and the flavors are blended, about 5 minutes longer.

Just before serving, add the green onions, bean sprouts, and lime juice. Remove the soup from the heat and season with salt and pepper to taste. Ladle into bowls and serve hot.

Serves 4

2 cups (16 fl oz/500 ml) unsweetened coconut milk

2 cups (16 fl oz/500 ml) Vegetable Stock (page 289) or broth

6 small dried red chiles, seeded

3 cloves garlic, crushed

1 lemongrass stalk, tops discarded and white bulb pounded flat, then cut into 1/2-inch (12-mm) slices

1/4 lb (125 g) small oyster mushrooms, brushed clean and stemmed

1 teaspoon finely grated lime zest

2 green (spring) onions, including the tender green tops, sliced

1/2 cup (1 oz/30 g) mung bean sprouts

Juice of 1 lime

Salt and freshly ground pepper

Spring Lettuces with Grapefruit and Sautéed Scallops

The tart, sweet taste of grapefruit is a refreshing counterpoint to the sweetness of plump scallops. Tarragon, with its own citrusy tones, is the ideal complement to the two flavors. Serve as part of a light spring menu.

2 grapefruits

1 tablespoon extra-virgin olive oil

2 tablespoons minced fresh tarragon, plus 4 sprigs for garnish

1 teaspoon minced shallot

3/4 teaspoon salt

4 cups (4 oz/125 g) mixed young, tender lettuces

12 sea scallops (about 3/4 lb/375 g)

1 tablespoon unsalted butter

1/2 teaspoon freshly ground pepper

Using a sharp knife, cut a slice off the top and bottom of 1 grapefruit to expose the flesh. Place the fruit upright on the cutting board and thickly slice off the peel in strips, cutting around the contour of the fruit to expose the flesh. Holding the grapefruit over a bowl, cut along either side of each section, letting the sections and any juice drop into the bowl. Remove any seeds and discard. Cut the sections into 1/2-inch (12-mm) pieces. Set aside. Juice the second grapefruit into another bowl.

Pour half of the grapefruit juice into a large bowl and add the olive oil, minced tarragon, shallot, and 1/2 teaspoon of the salt. Using a fork or spoon, mix well. Add the lettuces and the grapefruit pieces to the bowl and toss to mix well. Divide the mixture evenly among individual plates.

Pat the scallops dry with paper towels. In a frying pan over medium-high heat, melt the butter. When it is foaming, add the scallops and sauté until they begin to turn opaque on the bottom, about 1 minute. Sprinkle the scallops with the pepper and the remaining 1/4 teaspoon salt and turn them over. Continue to cook until opaque throughout and just lightly browned but still soft and tender, about 45 seconds longer.

Pour the remaining grapefruit juice over the scallops, reduce the heat to low, and deglaze the pan, stirring with a wooden spoon to scrape up any browned bits from the pan bottom. Using a slotted spatula, transfer the scallops to the salad greens, arranging them on top and dividing evenly. Drizzle the pan juices evenly over the tops. Garnish each plate with a tarragon sprig and serve immediately.

Serves 4

Warm Shrimp Salad with Salsa Verde

This brightly flavored salsa verde is a perfect dressing for warm poached shrimp. As an alternative to shrimp, substitute 2 pounds (1 kg) mussels or 3 pounds (1.5 kg) clams. The mussels will cook in 2–3 minutes, the clams in 3–5 minutes. Serve with a white wine.

To make the salsa verde, in a bowl, stir together the parsley, chives, thyme, oregano, capers, minced garlic, lemon juice, and olive oil. Season to taste with salt and pepper and set aside.

In a frying pan over medium heat, bring the clam juice to a boil. Add the shrimp, cover, and cook until they turn pink and begin to curl, 1–2 minutes. Using a slotted spoon, transfer the shrimp to a plate.

Raise the heat to high and boil the cooking liquid until it is reduced to 1–2 tablespoons, 1–2 minutes. Remove from the heat, let cool, then stir into the salsa verde.

As soon as the shrimp are cool enough to handle, peel them, discarding the shells, then devein. Add the shrimp to the salsa verde and toss to coat evenly.

Place the shrimp on a platter and garnish with the lemon wedges and chives. Split the wheat rolls and lightly toast. Rub the warm toasted rolls lightly with the whole garlic clove and serve immediately with the shrimp.

Serves 6

FOR THE SALSA VERDE:

1/3 cup (1/2 oz/15 g) chopped fresh flat-leaf (Italian) parsley

2 tablespoons chopped fresh chives

1/2 teaspoon chopped fresh thyme

1/4 teaspoon chopped fresh oregano

1/4 cup (2 oz/60 g) capers, chopped

2 cloves garlic minced

1/4 cup (2 fl oz/60 ml) fresh lemon juice

1/3 cup (3 fl oz/80 ml) extra-virgin olive oil

Salt and freshly ground pepper

1/2 cup (4 fl oz/125 ml) bottled clam juice or water

1 1/4 lb (625 g) shrimp (prawns)

6 lemon wedges

Fresh chives, for garnish

6 crusty wheat rolls

1 clove garlic, peeled

Tabbouleh

Bulgur and tomatoes are the main components of this Middle Eastern salad. Eat it by scooping it up with a fork, or, alternatively, capture it with wedges of pita bread. Tabbouleh is best when made at least 1 day in advance so that the flavors marry.

3/4 cup (4$^{1}/_{2}$ oz/140 g) medium-fine bulgur wheat

1 cup (8 fl oz/250 ml) lemon juice, or as needed

$^{1}/_{2}$ cup (4 fl oz/125 ml) extra-virgin olive oil

5 cloves garlic, minced

8 green (spring) onions, including the tender green tops, diced

1 cup (1$^{1}/_{2}$ oz/45 g) chopped fresh flat-leaf (Italian) parsley

$^{1}/_{3}$ cup ($^{1}/_{2}$ oz/15 g) chopped fresh mint

4 large, ripe tomatoes, diced

1 English (hothouse) cucumber, peeled, halved, seeded, and diced

2$^{1}/_{2}$ teaspoons salt

$^{1}/_{4}$ teaspoon freshly ground pepper

1 head romaine (cos) lettuce, leaves separated, or 3 pita bread rounds, heated and cut into wedges

Place the bulgur on the bottom of a large salad bowl. In a small bowl, whisk together the 1 cup (8 fl oz/250 ml) lemon juice, the olive oil, and garlic and drizzle over the bulgur. Layer the ingredients in the following order on top of the bulgur: green onions, parsley, mint, tomatoes, and cucumber. Season the top layer with 1$^{1}/_{2}$ teaspoons of the salt and the pepper and cover with plastic wrap. Refrigerate for at least 24 hours or for up to 48 hours.

To serve, bring the salad to room temperature and toss the ingredients together. Taste and season with the remaining 1 teaspoon salt and more lemon juice, if needed. Serve with the romaine leaves or warmed pita bread.

Serves 6

Pasta & Pizza

Cheese Ravioli with Tomato Sauce

Delicate homemade ravioli surpasses anything you can buy. Recruit a helper, if possible, to make the work go faster. To lighten your work load, purchase your favorite store-bought tomato sauce to toss into the freshly made ravioli.

FOR THE FILLING:

3/4 lb (375 g) whole-milk ricotta cheese

1½ cups (6 oz/185 g) grated Parmesan cheese

1 egg

¼ teaspoon ground nutmeg

Salt and freshly ground pepper

1 lb (500 g) Fresh Egg Pasta (page 289), rolled and cut into sheets

Semolina flour for dusting

2 cups (16 fl oz/500 ml) Classic Tomato Sauce (page 290) or purchased

To make the filling, in a bowl, combine the ricotta, ½ cup (2 oz/60 g) of the Parmesan cheese, the egg, and nutmeg. Mix well with a fork. Season to taste with salt and pepper. Cover and refrigerate until needed.

Working with 1 pasta sheet at a time, place on a work surface dusted with semolina flour, with the longer side of the pasta facing you. Measure the width of the pasta sheet (the shorter dimension) and divide by two to give you the size of the finished ravioli. Make notches along the long edge of the pasta sheet with a pastry wheel to mark each ravioli size. Put about 1½ teaspoons filling in the center of the ravioli on the bottom half of each pasta sheet. Moisten the dough edges lightly with water. Fold over the top half of the sheet, matching the edges. Press firmly between and around the ravioli to seal well. Using a fluted pastry wheel, cut between the ravioli. Transfer to the prepared baking sheets. You should have at least 4 dozen ravioli. Let the ravioli dry for 30 minutes at room temperature. (If you let them stand longer, cover with a kitchen towel to prevent further drying.)

Bring a large pot three-fourths full of salted water to a boil over high heat. Meanwhile, warm the tomato sauce over low heat until heated through; keep warm. Add the ravioli to the boiling water, stir gently, and then cook at a gentle boil until al dente (tender but firm to the bite), about 1½ minutes. Using a large sieve, transfer the ravioli to a warmed serving bowl. Add the sauce and toss gently.

Divide the ravioli among warmed bowls. Top each portion with the remaining 1 cup (4 oz/125 g) Parmesan cheese and serve at once.

Serves 4–6

Penne alla Norma

In a bowl, toss the eggplant cubes with 2 teaspoons salt. Transfer to a sieve or colander and let stand for 1 hour to drain.

In a large sauté pan over medium heat, warm 2 tablespoons of the olive oil. Add the garlic and red pepper flakes and sauté for 1 minute to release the garlic's fragrance. Add the tomatoes, raise the heat to medium-high, and simmer, stirring often, until the tomatoes break down and form a sauce, about 15 minutes. Add a little water if the sauce becomes too thick. Season to taste with salt, then stir in the basil. Remove from the heat.

Pat the eggplant with paper towels. In a large, nonstick sauté pan over medium-high heat, warm 1 tablespoon of the remaining olive oil. Add half of the eggplant and sauté until browned, about 10 minutes. Transfer to the pan holding the tomato sauce. Repeat with the remaining 1 tablespoon oil and the remaining eggplant.

Bring the eggplant and sauce to a simmer over medium heat, adding water if needed to thin the sauce. Cover and maintain a gentle simmer. Cook until the eggplant is soft but not mushy, 15–20 minutes. Remove from the heat.

Bring a large pot three-fourths full of salted water to a boil over high heat. Add the pasta, stir well, and cook until al dente (tender but firm to the bite), about 12 minutes or according to the package directions. While the pasta is cooking, reheat the sauce gently over low heat.

Drain the pasta, reserving about 1 cup (8 fl oz/250 ml) of the cooking water. Return the pasta to the warm pot. Add the sauce and toss. Add 1/4 cup (1 oz/30 g) of the pecorino and toss again, adding some of the reserved water if needed to thin the sauce. Divide among warmed dishes. Top with the remaining 1/4 cup (1 oz/30 g) pecorino cheese, dividing it evenly. Serve at once.

Serves 4–6

1 eggplant (aubergine), about 1 lb (500 g), cut into 3/4-inch (2-cm) cubes

2 teaspoons salt, plus more as needed

4 tablespoons (2 fl oz/60 ml) olive oil

3 cloves garlic, minced

Pinch of red pepper flakes

1 lb (500 g) ripe plum (Roma) tomatoes, diced

12 fresh basil leaves, torn into small pieces

1 lb (500 g) dried penne

1/2 cup (2 oz/60 g) grated pecorino cheese

Bucatini with Anchovy Sauce

For anchovy lovers, this sauce provides uncomplicated pleasure. The secret to success is not to cook the anchovies, but to let them dissolve in the residual heat of the pan.

1 lb (500 g) dried bucatini, perciatelli, or spaghetti

¼ cup (2 fl oz/60 ml) olive oil

4 large cloves garlic, minced

3 tablespoons minced fresh flat-leaf (Italian) parsley

8 anchovy fillets in olive oil, drained and chopped

Salt and freshly ground pepper

Bring a large pot three-fourths full of salted water to a boil over high heat. Add the pasta, stir well, and cook until al dente (tender but firm to the bite), about 12 minutes or according to the package directions.

While the pasta is cooking, in a large sauté pan over medium heat, warm the olive oil. Add the garlic and 2 tablespoons of the parsley and sauté for 1 minute to release the garlic's fragrance. Remove from the heat and add the anchovies. With the back of a wooden spoon, mash the anchovies until they dissolve into the oil. Season to taste with salt and pepper. Keep warm.

Using tongs, transfer the pasta, still dripping wet, to the sauté pan. (Alternatively, drain the pasta, leaving it dripping wet. Return to the warm pot and add the sauce.) Toss the pasta well with the sauce. Divide among warmed dishes. Top with the remaining 1 tablespoon parsley, dividing it evenly. Serve at once.

Serves 4–6

Penne with Swordfish, Tomatoes, Olives, and Capers

This seafood sauce hails from Sicily, which boasts some of the world's finest swordfish. Like most fish and shellfish sauces for pasta, it does not need cheese, though you can add it if you wish.

In a large sauté pan over medium heat, warm the olive oil. Add the garlic and red pepper flakes and sauté for 1 minute to release the garlic's fragrance. Add the tomatoes, oregano, and 1/2 cup (4 fl oz/125 ml) water. Raise the heat to medium-high, bring to a simmer, and cook, stirring often, until the tomatoes break down and form a sauce, about 15 minutes. Season to taste with salt. Reduce the heat, add the swordfish, cover, and simmer gently until the fish is opaque throughout, about 10 minutes.

Using a wooden spoon, mash the swordfish into the sauce, breaking it up until no large pieces remain. Stir in the olives, capers, and 1 tablespoon of the parsley. Remove from the heat.

Bring a large pot three-fourths full of salted water to a boil over high heat. Add the pasta, stir well, and cook until al dente (tender but firm to the bite), about 12 minutes or according to the package directions. While the pasta is cooking, reheat the sauce gently over low heat.

Drain the pasta and return it to the warm pot. Add the sauce and toss to mix well. Divide the sauced pasta among warmed dishes. Top with the remaining 1 tablespoon parsley, dividing it evenly. Serve at once.

Serves 4–6

1/4 cup (2 fl oz/60 ml) olive oil

3 cloves garlic, minced

1/8 teaspoon red pepper flakes

1 lb (500 g) ripe plum (Roma) tomatoes, peeled, seeded, and diced

2 teaspoons minced fresh oregano

Salt

3/4 lb (375 g) swordfish fillets, skin removed, cut into 1/2-inch (12-mm) dice

16 Kalamata olives or other Mediterranean brine-cured olives, pitted and quartered

1 tablespoon capers, rinsed, coarsely chopped if large

2 tablespoons minced fresh flat-leaf (Italian) parsley

1 lb (500 g) dried penne or spaghetti

Squash Flower and Black Olive Pasta

This brightly colored pasta can be made with the male or female flowers of summer squashes. The male flowers are usually sold in bunches like bouquets, while the female blossoms, which have immature squashes attached, are sold by the piece.

9 squash flowers

3/4 lb (375 g) penne, or other dried short pasta

1 tablespoon unsalted butter

3 tablespoons extra-virgin olive oil

1/2 yellow onion, chopped

3 cloves garlic, minced

10 oz (315 g) oil-cured black olives, pitted and halved (about 2 cups)

2 teaspoons minced fresh thyme

1 teaspoon salt

1 teaspoon freshly ground pepper

1/4 cup (1 oz/30 g) grated Parmesan cheese

Cut 8 of the squash flowers in half lengthwise. Remove and discard the furry anthers at their centers. Cut the flowers into long strips 1/4 inch (6 mm) wide and set aside. Reserve the remaining flower for garnish.

Bring a large pot three-fourths full of salted water to a boil over high heat. Add the pasta, stir well, and cook until al dente (tender but firm to the bite), about 12 minutes or according to the package directions.

Meanwhile, in a frying pan over medium heat, melt the butter with 1 tablespoon of the olive oil. Add the onion and garlic and sauté until translucent, 3–4 minutes. Add the olives and 1 teaspoon of the thyme. Continue to sauté until the olives become plump, 3–4 minutes longer.

Drain the pasta and place in a warmed serving bowl. Drizzle with the remaining 2 tablespoons olive oil, sprinkle with the salt and the pepper, and toss to coat evenly. Add the olive mixture and all the pan juices and toss to coat again. Finally, add the remaining 1 teaspoon thyme and the cut-up squash flowers and toss gently. Sprinkle with the Parmesan cheese and garnish with the remaining whole squash flower. Serve at once.

Serves 4

Pad Thai

Place the noodles in a bowl, add warm water to cover, and let soak until soft and pliable, about 15 minutes. Drain and set aside.

Cut the chicken into strips ⅛ inch (3 mm) thick. In a nonstick wok or frying pan over medium-high heat, warm 1 tablespoon of the oil. Add the chicken and toss and stir until opaque throughout, about 1 minute. Add the shrimp and toss and stir until bright pink, about 1 minute longer. Transfer to a bowl and set aside.

Return the wok to medium-high heat and add the remaining 1 tablespoon oil. Add the garlic and shallots and toss and stir until golden, about 1 minute. Raise the heat to high and add the tomato paste, fish sauce, lime juice, and sugar. Toss and stir until thickened, about 30 seconds. Break the egg into the middle of the wok, lightly beat, and cook, without stirring, until set, about 20 seconds. Gently fold the egg into the sauce; tiny egg flecks should peek through the sauce. Add the noodles and red pepper flakes and, using tongs, toss to coat with the sauce. Add the stock, 2 tablespoons at a time, to moisten the stiff noodles, and cook until the noodles begin to cling together and are almost tender, about 3 minutes. Add the bean sprouts, green onions, carrot, chicken-shrimp mixture, and half of the peanuts. Toss to combine and cook until the bean sprouts begin to wilt, about 3 minutes.

Divide the ingredients among individual plates and top with the remaining peanuts and the cilantro. Squeeze the lime wedges over the noodles. Serve at once.

Serves 6

½ lb (250 g) dried rice ribbon noodles

1 skinless, boneless chicken breast half, about ¼ lb (125 g)

2 tablespoons vegetable oil

¼ lb (125 g) medium shrimp (prawns), peeled and deveined

3 cloves garlic, minced

¼ cup (1½ oz/45 g) minced shallots or yellow onion

3 tablespoons tomato paste

2 tablespoons Thai fish sauce, plus 1½ teaspoons

2 tablespoons lime juice

1 tablespoon sugar

1 egg

Pinch of red pepper flakes

¼ cup (2 fl oz/60 ml) Chicken Stock (page 288) or broth

½ lb (250 g) mung bean sprouts

6 green (spring) onions, including the tender green tops, cut into 2-inch (5-cm) pieces

1 carrot, peeled and julienned

⅓ cup (2½ oz/75 g) chopped roasted peanuts

½ cup (½ oz/15 g) fresh cilantro (fresh coriander) leaves

1 lime, cut into 6 wedges

Spicy Macaroni and Cheese

Adding fresh, spicy, green chiles gives this old-fashioned favorite new life. Serve with a salad of lettuce, tomato, and red onion and a light vinaigrette. Use cracker crumbs here, rather than dried bread crumbs, for a buttery, crisp crust.

3 small fresh poblano chiles or ¼ cup canned chopped green chiles

¼ cup fine cracker crumbs

2 tablespoons unsalted butter

2 teaspoons all-purpose (plain) flour

2 cups (16 fl oz/750 ml) whole milk, plus more as needed

¼ teaspoon salt

Pinch of red pepper flakes

1 lb (500 g) dried fusilli

4 cups (4 oz/125 g) finely shredded Cheddar cheese

If using fresh chiles, preheat the broiler (grill). Place the chiles on a baking sheet and broil (grill), turning as needed, until the skins blacken and blister. Remove from the broiler, cover loosely with aluminum foil, let cool for 10 minutes, then peel away the skins and remove the stem and seeds. Chop the chiles and set aside. Reduce the oven temperature to 350°F (180°C).

Bring a large pot three-fourths full of salted water to a boil over high heat.

Meanwhile, put the cracker crumbs in a small bowl. In a small saucepan over medium-low heat, melt the butter and add 1 teaspoon to the bowl and stir to coat.

Add the flour to the butter remaining in the saucepan and cook, whisking, until well blended, about 1 minute. Whisk in 2 cups (16 fl oz/750 ml) of the milk and add the salt, red pepper flakes, and chopped chiles. Cook, whisking constantly, until the mixture comes to a simmer and thickens, about 3 minutes. Reduce the heat to low and continue to cook, whisking occasionally, while you prepare the pasta. The sauce should be pourable; if it gets too thick, add a little more milk.

Add the pasta to the boiling water and cook for 5 minutes; it will be underdone. Drain and return the pasta to the warmed pot. Add the sauce and all but 2 tablespoons of the cheese. Stir until the cheese melts. Transfer to small individual baking dishes; an oval 8-by-5-inch (20-by-13-cm) gratin dish works well. Top with the remaining cheese and then with the cracker crumbs.

Bake until bubbling hot, 15–20 minutes. Let cool for a few minutes, then serve.

Serves 4

Linguine with Clams

Parsley, garlic, and red pepper flakes give this clam sauce its fresh, lively character. The best clams for this classic pasta are manila clams or littlenecks, though you may also use cherrystones. Pick the smallest you can find: they are the most tender.

Discard any clams that do not close to the touch, then scrub the clams well under running cold water. In a large pot, combine the wine and 1/2 cup (4 fl oz/125 ml) water. Bring to a simmer, add the clams, cover, and cook, shaking the pot once or twice to redistribute the clams, just until the clams open, about 3 minutes. Using a slotted spoon, transfer the clams to a bowl, discarding any that failed to open. Line a fine-mesh sieve with a triple thickness of cheesecloth (muslin) and pour the cooking liquid through it into a pitcher or bowl. Set the clams and strained liquid aside.

In a large sauté pan over medium heat, warm the olive oil. Add the onion and sauté until soft, about 10 minutes. Add the garlic, parsley, and red pepper flakes and sauté for 1 minute to release the garlic's fragrance. Remove from the heat.

Meanwhile, bring a large pot three-fourths full of salted water to a boil over high heat. Add the pasta, stir well, and cook until al dente (tender but firm to the bite), about 10 minutes or according to the package directions. Just before the pasta is done, add the strained clam liquid to the sauté pan and reheat over medium heat. Season to taste with salt. Reduce the heat to low, add the clams, and reheat gently.

Drain the pasta and return to the warm pot. Add the sauce and toss well. Divide among warmed bowls and serve at once.

Serves 4–6

4 dozen small clams, about 2 lb (1 kg) (see note), scrubbed

1/2 cup (4 fl oz/125 ml) dry white wine

1/4 cup (2 fl oz/60 ml) olive oil

1 small yellow onion, minced

4 cloves garlic, minced

1/4 cup (1/3 oz/10 g) minced fresh flat-leaf (Italian) parsley

1/4 teaspoon red pepper flakes

1 lb (500 g) dried linguine

Salt

Fettuccine with Brie and Asparagus

When small pieces of Brie are tossed with warm strands of fettuccine, the cheese melts to form a delectable sauce. Sautéed thinly sliced asparagus and chopped pistachio nuts add vivid color and texture.

1 lb (500 g) asparagus spears

3 tablespoons unsalted butter

1/2 cup (2 oz/60 g) unsalted pistachios, coarsely chopped

4 teaspoons grated lemon zest

1 lb (500 g) fresh or dried fettuccine

1/2 lb (250 g) Brie cheese, rind trimmed and cheese broken into small pieces

1/2 cup (2 oz/60 g) grated Parmesan cheese

Salt and freshly ground pepper

3 tablespoons chopped fresh flat-leaf (Italian) parsley

Bring a large pot three-fourths full of salted water to a boil over high heat.

While the water is heating, prepare the asparagus: Snap off the tough ends where they break naturally and discard. Starting at the base, cut the spears crosswise on a slight diagonal into sections $^{1}/8$ inch (3 mm) thick, leaving the tips whole.

In a large, heavy frying pan over medium-high heat, melt the butter. When hot, add the asparagus and cook, stirring constantly, until just tender, about 3 minutes. Remove from the heat and stir in the pistachios and lemon zest. Keep warm.

Add the pasta to the boiling water, stir well, and cook until al dente (tender but firm to the bite), 2–3 minutes for fresh pasta or about 12 minutes, or according to the package directions, for dried pasta. Drain, reserving $^{1}/3$ cup (3 fl oz/ 80 ml) of the cooking water, and return the pasta to the warm pot.

Immediately add the Brie and Parmesan cheeses and the reserved asparagus mixture. Stir and toss well to combine the melting cheeses with the pasta. Add the reserved cooking water to the pasta as needed to moisten. Season to taste with salt and pepper.

Transfer the pasta to a warmed large serving bowl and sprinkle with the parsley. Serve at once.

Serves 4

Fettuccine with Artichokes, Prosciutto, and Cream

Fettuccini, and other types of ribbon pasta, are typically served with cream or butter sauces, which nicely coat the wide strands. Since this pasta is so rich, round out the menu with a light starter and dessert.

Fill a bowl three-fourths full of water and add the lemon juice. Working with 1 artichoke at a time, break off the tough outer leaves, until you reach the pale yellow-green inner leaves. Cut off about 1 inch (2.5 cm) from the top of the artichoke. Cut off the stem flush with the bottom. Drop the trimmed artichokes into the lemon water and put an inverted plate in the bowl to keep them submerged. Bring a large pot three-fourths full of salted water to a boil over high heat.

In a large sauté pan over medium heat, warm the olive oil. Add the onion and sauté until softened, about 5 minutes. Meanwhile, halve the artichokes and slice thinly lengthwise. Add them to the pan along with 1/2 cup (4 fl oz/125 ml) of the stock. Season to taste with salt and pepper. Bring to a simmer over medium-high heat, cover, and adjust the heat to maintain a gentle simmer. Cook until the artichokes are tender, about 15 minutes. Uncover and add the remaining 1/2 cup stock and the cream. Return to a simmer and cook, uncovered, until the mixture thickens slightly. Stir in the prosciutto and parsley. Taste and adjust the seasonings. Remove from the heat, but keep warm.

Add the pasta to the boiling water. Stir well and cook until al dente (tender but firm to the bite), 2–3 minutes for fresh pasta or about 12 minutes or according to the package directions, for dried pasta. Drain the pasta, reserving about 1 cup (8 fl oz/ 250 ml) of the cooking water. Return the pasta to the warm pot. Add the sauce and toss, adding some of the reserved cooking water if needed to thin the sauce. Divide among warmed dishes and serve at once.

Serves 4–6

Juice of 1 lemon

16 small artichokes, about 2 oz (60 g) each

2 tablespoons olive oil

1/2 yellow onion, chopped

1 cup (8 fl oz/250 ml) Chicken Stock (page 288) or broth

Salt and freshly ground pepper

1 cup (8 fl oz/250 ml) heavy (double) cream

2 oz (60 g) prosciutto, minced

2 tablespoons minced fresh flat-leaf (Italian) parsley

1 lb (500 g) fresh or dried fettuccine

Penne with Sautéed Radicchio, Fennel, and Prosciutto

An Italian winter favorite, Treviso radicchio is an elongated variety with thick, white midribs. Like other radicchio, it turns brown when cooked, but has an extraordinary flavor. Here, it is sautéed with pale green fennel in an easy pasta dish.

Trim away the tough stems from each radicchio head, then cut them lengthwise into pieces $1/2$ inch (12 mm) wide. Cut off the stems, feathery tops, and bruised outer stalks from the fennel bulb, then cut lengthwise into julienne strips $1/4$ inch (6 mm) thick.

In a frying pan over medium-high heat, melt the butter with the 2 tablespoons olive oil. When the butter foams, add the garlic and sauté until translucent, 2–3 minutes. Add the radicchio and fennel and $1/2$ teaspoon each of the salt and pepper. Reduce the heat to low and sauté, stirring often, until the fennel is translucent and tender and the radicchio is lightly browned, about 10 minutes.

Meanwhile, bring a large pot three-fourths full of salted water to a boil over high heat. Add the pasta, stir well, and cook until al dente (tender but firm to the bite), about 12 minutes or according to the package directions.

Drain the pasta and transfer to a warmed serving bowl. Add the radicchio-fennel mixture and toss to coat evenly.

In the same frying pan over medium heat, warm the 1 teaspoon olive oil. Add the prosciutto and sauté just long enough to heat through, 1–2 minutes. Add the mixture to the pasta and toss to distribute evenly. Add the remaining $1/2$ teaspoon each salt and pepper and the thyme. Toss to mix, garnish with the Parmesan cheese, if desired, and serve at once.

Serves 4–6

2 heads Treviso or regular radicchio, about 1 lb (500 g) total weight

1 fennel bulb

2 tablespoons unsalted butter

2 tablespoons olive oil, plus 1 teaspoon

3 cloves garlic, chopped

1 teaspoon salt

1 teaspoon freshly ground pepper

3/4 lb (375 g) penne

1/4 lb (125 g) prosciutto or Virginia ham, cut into long, narrow strips

1 tablespoon minced fresh thyme

Shaved or grated Parmesan cheese for garnish (optional)

Butternut Squash Agnolotti with Butter and Sage

FOR THE FILLING:

1 small butternut squash, about 1½ lb (750 g), halved lengthwise, seeds and strings removed

1 egg, lightly beaten

¼ cup (1 oz/30 g) lightly toasted fine fresh bread crumbs

⅓ cup (1½ oz/45 g) grated Parmesan cheese

Salt

Freshly grated nutmeg

1 lb (500 g) Fresh Egg Pasta (page 289), rolled and cut into sheets

Semolina flour for dusting

2 tablespoons unsalted butter

2 tablespoons olive oil

36 large fresh sage leaves

Salt and freshly ground pepper

1 cup (4 oz/120 g) grated Parmesan cheese

To make the filling, preheat the oven to 375°F (190°C). Cut each squash half into 10–12 chunks. Place in a baking dish in a single layer. Add the ¼ cup (2 fl oz/ 60 ml) water and cover with aluminum foil. Bake the squash until tender, about 40 minutes. Let cool, then scoop the flesh from the skin and transfer the flesh to a food processor; discard the skin. Purée until smooth. Transfer 1 cup (8 fl oz/250 ml) of the purée to a bowl and stir in the egg, bread crumbs, and Parmesan cheese. Season with salt and nutmeg to taste. Cover and refrigerate until needed.

Working with 1 pasta sheet at a time, place on a work surface dusted with semolina flour. Using a round, fluted 3-inch (7.5-cm) cookie cutter, cut out as many rounds as possible. Put ½ teaspoon of the squash filling in the center of each round, moisten the edges lightly with water, then fold in half and press firmly to seal. Transfer to the prepared baking sheets. Let the agnolotti dry for 30 minutes at room temperature. (If you let them stand longer, cover with a kitchen towel to prevent further drying.)

Bring a large pot three-fourths full of salted water to a boil over high heat. Meanwhile, in a large sauté pan over medium heat, melt the butter with the olive oil. Add the sage leaves, reduce the heat to low, and cook, turning each leaf occasionally, until they begin to crisp, 7–8 minutes. Transfer to paper towels to drain. Reserve the oil and butter in the pan. Add the agnolotti to the boiling water, stir gently, and cook at a gentle boil until al dente (tender but firm to the bite), about 2 minutes. Using a large sieve, transfer the agnolotti to a warmed serving bowl. Add the reserved oil and butter; season to taste with salt and pepper, and toss gently to coat with the seasonings. Add ½ cup (2 oz/60 g) of the Parmesan cheese and the fried sage leaves and gently toss again. Serve at once. Pass the remaining ½ cup (2 oz/ 60 g) Parmesan cheese at the table.

Serves 4–6

Rigatoni with Sweet Peppers

Sweet bell peppers (capsicums), slowly cooked, render substantial juices that transform them into a flavorful sauce. Using peppers of different colors makes the most beautiful dish, but it isn't essential.

¼ cup (2 fl oz/60 ml) olive oil

1 small yellow onion, halved and thinly sliced

2 cloves garlic, minced

Pinch of red pepper flakes

3 bell peppers (capsicums), 1 *each* red, yellow, and green, halved, seeded, and thinly sliced lengthwise

1 tablespoon minced fresh oregano

Salt

20 Kalamata olives or other brine-cured Mediterranean-style olives, pitted and quartered

1 lb (500 g) dried rigatoni or spaghetti

½ cup (2 oz/60 g) grated pecorino cheese

In a large sauté pan over medium heat, warm the olive oil. Add the onion and sauté until softened, about 5 minutes. Add the garlic and red pepper flakes and sauté for 1 minute to release the garlic's fragrance. Add the bell peppers and oregano and season generously with salt. Stir to coat with the seasonings, then cover and adjust the heat so the peppers cook without burning. Cook until the peppers are soft and juicy, about 20 minutes. Stir in the olives and remove from the heat.

Bring a large pot three-fourths full of salted water to a boil over high heat. Add the pasta, stir well, and cook until al dente (tender but firm to the bite), 10–12 minutes or according to the package directions. While the pasta is cooking, reheat the sauce gently over low heat.

Drain the pasta and return to the warm pot. Add the sauce and toss to mix well. Divide the sauced pasta among warmed dishes and serve at once. Pass the pecorino cheese at the table.

Serves 4–6

Farfalle with Peas and Prosciutto

If you are fortunate enough to find fresh peas, you can substitute shelled, small fresh peas for the frozen peas. Vegetarians can leave out the prosciutto, and the results will still be delicious.

In a large sauté pan over medium heat, warm the olive oil. Add the onion and sauté until it is soft and beginning to caramelize, about 15 minutes. Add the peas and $^{1}/_{2}$ cup (4 fl oz/125 ml) water, and season to taste with salt and pepper. Bring to a simmer and cook, uncovered, stirring often, until the peas are tender, about 5 minutes. Remove from the heat.

Bring a large pot three-fourths full of salted water to a boil over high heat. Add the pasta, stir well, and cook until al dente (tender but firm to the bite), about 12 minutes or according to the package directions. While the pasta is cooking, reheat the pea mixture gently over low heat. Stir in the prosciutto and parsley.

Drain the pasta and return to the warm pot. Add the butter and toss until it melts. Add the pea mixture and toss again. Divide among warmed dishes. Top each portion with a little of the Parmesan cheese. Pass the remaining Parmesan cheese at the table.

Serves 4–6

2 tablespoons olive oil

1 large yellow onion, halved and thinly sliced

1 package (10 oz/315 g) frozen petite peas, or 2 cups (10 oz/315 g) shelled small fresh peas

Salt and freshly ground pepper

1 lb (500 g) dried farfalle

2 oz (60 g) prosciutto, minced

2 tablespoons minced fresh flat-leaf (Italian) parsley

2 tablespoons unsalted butter, at room temperature

$^{3}/_{4}$ cup (3 oz/90 g) grated Parmesan cheese

Pizza with Tomatoes, Olives, and Pancetta

Make the pizza dough. Toward the end of the rising time, position oven racks in the middle and lower third of the oven and preheat it to 450°F (230°C). Lightly grease 2 baking sheets.

When the dough has risen to double in bulk, punch it down and divide it in half. On a lightly floured work surface, roll out each half into a very thin 12-inch (30 cm) round. Fold over the outer $^1/_2$-inch (12-mm) edge of each round and pinch it to make a rim. Prick the rounds all over with the tines of a fork and place on the prepared baking sheets. (If desired, cover with plastic wrap, and then with aluminum foil, and refrigerate for up to 1 day. Bring to room temperature for 30 minutes before baking.)

To make the topping, in a large frying pan over medium-low heat, cook the pancetta slices, turning occasionally, until crisp, 5–6 minutes. Transfer to paper towels to drain. When cool, crumble the pancetta and set aside. In a bowl, toss together the tomatoes, vinegar, and red pepper flakes.

Bake the pizza crusts for 5 minutes to crisp slightly, then remove from the oven. Spread each warm crust with half of the goat cheese, then top each with half of the tomato mixture. Sprinkle each pizza with half each of the olives, pancetta, dried basil, oregano, and fontina cheese. Drizzle each pizza with $1^1/_2$–2 tablespoons olive oil.

Return the pizzas to the oven and bake until the cheese melts atnd the crusts are crisp, 5–8 minutes. Remove from the oven and sprinkle each pizza with 2 tablespoons of the fresh basil. Cut each pizza into 6 wedges and serve immediately.

Serves 4–6

Basic Pizza Dough (page 291)

FOR THE TOPPING:

12–16 thin pancetta slices

10 plum (Roma) tomatoes, halved, seeded, and cut into wedges

2 teaspoons balsamic vinegar

2 generous pinches of red pepper flakes

6 oz (185 g) fresh, creamy goat cheese

30 Kalamata olives, pitted and sliced

1 teaspoon dried basil

1 teaspoon dried oregano

1 cup (4 oz/125 g) shredded fontina cheese

About 1/4 cup (2 fl oz/60 ml) extra-virgin olive oil

1/4 cup (1/2 oz/15 g) julienned fresh basil leaves

Linguine alla Carbonara

Be sure to serve this classic Roman pasta on warmed dishes to keep it warm longer. The heat of the pasta partially cooks the eggs. Note, however, that many health professionals advise against serving eggs that are not fully cooked.

4 eggs

3/4 cup (3 oz/90 g) grated Parmesan cheese

2 tablespoons minced fresh flat-leaf (Italian) parsley

1 teaspoon coarsely cracked pepper

1/2 teaspoon salt

1 lb (500 g) dried linguine

1 tablespoon olive oil

1 tablespoon unsalted butter

1/4 lb (125 g) pancetta, coarsely chopped

2 cloves garlic, minced

Bring a large pot three-fourths full of salted water to a boil over high heat. Meanwhile, in a large bowl, combine the eggs, Parmesan cheese, parsley, pepper, and salt. Whisk to blend.

Add the pasta to the boiling water, stir well, and cook until al dente (tender but firm to the bite), about 10 minutes or according to the package directions.

While the pasta is cooking, combine the olive oil, butter, pancetta, and garlic in a sauté pan over medium heat and cook, stirring occasionally, until the pancetta renders some of its fat, about 3 minutes; do not let it become crisp. Keep warm over low heat.

Using tongs, transfer the pasta, still dripping wet, to the bowl with the egg mixture. Toss immediately to coat with egg. Add the contents of the sauté pan and continue tossing until the egg coats the pasta evenly in creamy sauce. Add a little of the pasta cooking water if needed to thin the sauce. Divide among warmed dishes. Serve at once.

Serves 4–6

Angel Hair Pasta with Spring Vegetables

The best seasonal vegetables star in this simple pasta dish. Blanching the vegetables helps them retain their brilliant colors. The angel hair pasta, also known as capellini, is very thin and cooks quickly, so be careful not to overcook it.

Shell the fava beans. Have ready a bowl of ice water. Bring a saucepan three-fourths full of water to a boil. Add the beans and boil for 2 minutes, then drain. Transfer the beans to the ice water, then drain. Squeeze each bean free of its tough outer skin. If the beans are very small, they can be left unskinned. Set aside.

Ready a fresh bowl of ice water. Refill the saucepan three-fourths full with lightly salted water and bring to a boil. Add the carrots, boil for 2 minutes, and remove them with a slotted spoon. Immerse immediately in the ice water to stop the cooking, then scoop out and set aside. Repeat with the asparagus, cooking for 1 minute, and the snap peas, cooking for 30 seconds.

Bring a large pot three-fourths full of salted water to a boil over high heat. Add the pasta, stir well, and cook until al dente (tender but firm to the bite), 3–4 minutes or according to the package directions. Drain and transfer to a warmed bowl. Toss with 3 tablespoons of the olive oil. Keep warm.

Meanwhile, in a sauté pan over medium heat, warm the remaining 3 tablespoons olive oil. Add the onion and sauté until golden brown, 5–7 minutes. Add the stock and bring to a boil. Boil until reduced by one-half, 10–15 minutes. Add the carrots, asparagus, snap peas, and fava beans. Heat until the vegetables are warmed through and just tender, 3–4 minutes. Season to taste with salt and pepper.

Toss the vegetable mixture with the pasta, turn into a warmed serving bowl, and scatter the tomatoes and basil on top. Sprinkle with the Parmesan cheese and serve.

Serves 6

2 lb (1 kg) fava (broad) beans, shelled

1 bunch baby carrots (about 6 oz/185 g), trimmed, peeled, and halved lengthwise

1/2 lb (250 g) asparagus spears, tough ends removed, cut into 2-inch (5-cm) lengths

1/2 lb (250 g) sugar snap peas, trimmed

1 lb (500 g) dried angel hair pasta

6 tablespoons (3 fl oz/90 ml) olive oil

1 yellow onion, diced

3 cups (24 fl oz/750 ml) Vegetable Stock (page 289) or broth

Salt and freshly ground pepper

1 cup (6 oz/185 g) yellow pear cherry tomatoes, halved lengthwise

1/2 cup (1/2 oz/15 g) fresh basil leaves, shredded

2 oz (60 g) Parmesan cheese, grated

Pappardelle with Chicken, Caramelized Onions, and Rosemary

About 6 tablespoons (3 fl oz/ 105 ml) olive oil

4¹/₂ cups (1 lb/500 g) thinly sliced yellow onions

¹/₂ teaspoon sugar

2¹/₂ lb (1.25 kg) skinless, boneless, chicken breasts, cut into 1-inch (2.5-cm) cubes

1 tablespoon chopped garlic

3 tablespoons all-purpose (plain) flour

3 tablespoons finely chopped fresh rosemary

¹/₂ teaspoon salt, plus more as needed

¹/₄ teaspoon freshly ground pepper

3 cups (24 fl oz/750 ml) Chicken Stock (page 288) or broth

1 cup (8 fl oz/250 ml) dry white wine

3 fresh flat-leaf (Italian) parsley sprigs, plus ¹/₂ cup (³/₄ oz/20 g) chopped parsley

1¹/₄ lb (625 g) dried pappardelle

1 tablespoon unsalted butter

6 oz (185 g) fresh goat cheese, crumbled

1 tablespoon grated lemon zest

In a large, heavy, deep-sided pot over medium heat, warm 2 tablespoons of the olive oil. When hot, add the onions and sugar and cook, stirring constantly, until the onions are limp and golden brown, about 15 minutes. Transfer to a plate.

Add 2 tablespoons of the oil to the same pot and place over medium-high heat. Working in 2 batches, add only enough chicken to make a single layer and cook, turning often, until browned, 2–3 minutes longer. Using a slotted spoon, transfer the chicken to a plate. Repeat to brown all the chicken, adding more oil as needed.

Return the browned chicken to the pot and place over medium-high heat. Add the garlic and stir until fragrant, about 1 minute. Sprinkle the chicken with the flour and toss well. Add 2¹/₂ tablespoons of the rosemary, the ¹/₂ teaspoon salt, and the pepper and stir to combine. Stir in the stock, wine, the parsley sprigs, and the caramelized onions and bring to a simmer. Reduce the heat to low and cook, uncovered, until the chicken is fork tender, about 45 minutes. Taste and adjust the seasonings. Remove and discard the parsley sprigs.

Just before the chicken is ready, bring a large pot three-fourths full of salted water to a boil over high heat. Add the pasta, stir well, and cook until al dente (tender, but firm to the bite), about 12 minutes or according to the package directions. Drain and return to the warm pot. Add the butter and salt to taste and toss well.

To serve, divide the pasta among warmed individual plates and ladle the chicken-onion mixture on top, dividing evenly. Sprinkle each serving with equal amounts of the goat cheese, lemon zest, chopped parsley, and the remaining ¹/₂ tablespoon rosemary. Serve at once.

Serves 6

Orecchiette with Broccoli and Pine Nuts

This recipe uses both the broccoli florets and the stems. For best results, choose broccoli with thin stems, which will be more tender. To make a more substantial dish, add 2 ounces (60 g) bulk pork sausage, browning it along with the garlic.

In a small, dry frying pan over medium-low heat, combine the pine nuts and 1 tablespoon of the olive oil. Cook, stirring constantly, until the nuts are golden brown, about 5 minutes. Pour onto a small plate and set aside.

Separate the broccoli florets from the stems. Using a small sharp knife, peel the stems thickly to reveal the pale green heart. Bring a large pot three-fourths full of salted water to a boil over high heat. Add the broccoli florets and stems and cook until both are just tender when pierced with the tip of a sharp knife. The florets will cook in about 3 minutes, while the stems may take 5–6 minutes. Using tongs, lift out the broccoli pieces and drain in a sieve. Chop coarsely.

Add the pasta to the same boiling water, stir well, and cook until al dente (tender but firm to the bite), about 11 minutes or according to the package directions.

While the pasta is cooking, heat the remaining 4 tablespoons olive oil in a frying pan over medium heat. Add the garlic and red pepper flakes and sauté for 1 minute to release their fragrance. Add the broccoli and pine nuts, season generously with salt, and stir to coat with the seasonings. Cook until the broccoli is heated through.

Drain the pasta, reserving about 1/4 cup (2 fl oz/60 ml) of the cooking water. Return the pasta to the warm pot. Add the broccoli mixture and toss, adding a tablespoon or two of the cooking water if needed to moisten the pasta. Transfer to a warmed serving bowl and serve at once.

Serves 4

1/4 cup pine nuts

5 tablespoons extra-virgin olive oil

2 lb (1 kg) broccoli

1 lb (500 g) dried orecchiette

4 cloves garlic, minced

1 tablespoon red pepper flakes

Salt

Fettuccine with Cherry Tomatoes, Arugula, and Bread Crumbs

Everybody needs a repertoire of 10-minute pasta sauces such as this one. Make it in the summer when cherry tomatoes are at their best. If you can not find arugula (rocket), substitute 12 fresh basil leaves. Add them to the sauce when you add the pasta.

1 cup (½ oz/15 g) fine fresh bread crumbs

2 teaspoons, olive oil, plus 2 tablespoons

4 large cloves garlic, minced

2½ cups (15 oz/470 g) cherry tomatoes, stemmed and halved

Salt and freshly ground pepper

6 cups (6 oz/185 g) arugula (rocket), coarsely chopped

1 lb (500 g) fresh or dried fettuccine

Preheat the oven to 325°F (165°C). Put the bread crumbs in a pie pan or on a rimmed baking sheet and bake until golden brown, about 10 minutes. Transfer to a bowl and toss with the 2 teaspoons olive oil until evenly coated. Set aside.

Bring a large pot three-fourths full of salted water to a boil over high heat.

Meanwhile, in a large frying pan over medium heat, combine the 2 tablespoons olive oil, the garlic, and cherry tomatoes. Cook gently until the tomatoes release some of their juices, about 2 minutes. Do not allow the tomatoes to collapse completely. Season to taste with salt and pepper and stir in the arugula. Cook just until the arugula wilts slightly—it will wilt more in the heat of the pasta—then reduce the heat to low and keep warm.

Add the pasta to the boiling water, stir well, and cook until al dente (tender but firm to the bite), 1–2 minutes for fresh pasta and about 12 minutes or according to the package directions, for dried. Drain and transfer to the frying pan. Toss to coat well with the sauce.

Transfer the sauced pasta to a warmed serving bowl. Top with the fresh toasted bread crumbs, and serve at once.

Serves 4

Polenta Lasagna with Gorgonzola Sauce

To make the polenta, preheat the oven to 375°F (190°C). Lightly oil a baking sheet.

In a sauté pan over medium heat, warm the olive oil. Add the garlic and sauté until softened, 2–3 minutes. Add the mushrooms and eggplant and cook, stirring occasionally, until the liquid evaporates, 10–12 minutes. Stir in the parsley, season to taste with salt and pepper, and set aside.

In a saucepan over high heat, bring 4 1/2 cups (36 fl oz/1.1 l) water to a boil. Slowly add the polenta, stirring constantly. Reduce the heat to medium and continue to cook, stirring constantly, until the polenta pulls away from the pan sides, about 20 minutes. Remove from the heat and stir in the mushroom mixture. Spread the polenta about 1/2 inch (12 mm) thick on the prepared baking sheet, smoothing the top. Bake until firm and lightly browned, about 15 minutes. Let cool completely on the baking sheet.

To make the sauce, melt the butter in a heavy saucepan over medium heat. Add the flour and cook, stirring, until incorporated, 2–3 minutes. Slowly add the milk, whisking constantly, until smooth. Simmer, stirring often, until thickened, about 10 minutes. Add the Gorgonzola and thyme and stir until the cheese melts. Season to taste with salt and pepper. Remove from the heat.

Lightly oil a 9-by-13-inch (23-by-33-cm) baking dish. To assemble the lasagna, peel and thinly slice the tomatoes. Coarsely grate the zucchini. Spoon enough of the sauce into the prepared baking dish to cover the bottom lightly. Cut a piece of polenta to fit the bottom of the dish and place it on the sauce. Arrange half of the tomato slices in a layer on top and then half of the zucchini. Top with half of the remaining sauce. Cover with the remaining polenta, tomato slices, zucchini, and finally the remaining sauce. Bake until heated through, about 30 minutes. Cut into squares and serve hot.

Serves 8

FOR THE VEGETABLE POLENTA:

2 tablespoons olive oil

4 cloves garlic, minced

1/2 lb (250 g) fresh mushrooms, brushed clean, and sliced

1 eggplant (aubergine), 1/2 lb (250 g), peeled and diced

2 tablespoons minced fresh flat-leaf (Italian) parsley

Salt and freshly ground pepper

1 1/2 cups (7 1/2 oz/235 g) polenta

FOR THE GORGONZOLA SAUCE:

1/2 cup (4 oz/125 g) unsalted butter

6 tablespoons (2 oz/60 g) all-purpose (plain) flour

3 cups (24 fl oz/750 ml) whole milk, heated

3 oz (90 g) Gorgonzola cheese, crumbled

1 teaspoon minced fresh thyme

Salt and freshly ground pepper

2 tomatoes

2 zucchini (courgettes)

Spinach Lasagna

To make the béchamel sauce, melt the butter in a saucepan over medium heat. Add the flour and whisk to blend. Cook, whisking constantly, for 1 minute. Add the milk and bring to a simmer, whisking. Add the thyme and bay leaf and season to taste with nutmeg, salt, and pepper. Reduce the heat to low and cook gently, whisking often, until thickened, about 30 minutes. Press the sauce through a coarse-mesh sieve into a bowl; let cool.

Preheat the oven to 400°F (200°C). Fill a large bowl three-fourths full of ice water and add the olive oil. Bring a large pot three-fourths full of salted water to a boil over high heat. Cook the pasta sheets, 2 sheets at a time, for 10 seconds only. Transfer to the ice water and unfurl the sheets in the water, then lay flat on a kitchen towel and pat dry.

Pour a thin layer of the cooled béchamel sauce into a 9-by-13-inch (23-by-33-cm) baking dish. Top with a layer of pasta, cutting the sheets to fit. Spread 3 tablespoons béchamel sauce thinly and evenly over the pasta, then spread about 1/3 cup (3 fl oz/ 80 ml) of the meat sauce thinly over the béchamel. Sprinkle with a generous tablespoon of the Parmesan. Continue making layers of pasta, béchamel, meat sauce, and Parmesan until you use up all the sauces, reserving 1/3 cup béchamel and 2 tablespoons Parmesan cheese. You should have enough to make 10–12 layers of pasta and sauce. Finish with a layer of pasta topped with the reserved béchamel sauce. Sprinkle the 2 tablespoons of the Parmesan cheese evenly over the top.

Bake the lasagna, uncovered, until puffed and bubbling, 25–30 minutes. If desired, place under a preheated broiler (grill) briefly to brown the surface. Let cool for 15 minutes, then cut into squares to serve.

Serves 6–8

FOR THE BÉCHAMEL SAUCE:

4 tablespoons (2 oz/60 g) unsalted butter

1/4 cup (1 1/2 oz/45 g) all-purpose (plain) flour

3 cups (24 fl oz/750 ml) whole milk

4 fresh thyme sprigs

1 bay leaf

Freshly grated nutmeg

Salt and freshly ground pepper

1 lb (500 g) Fresh Spinach Pasta (290), rolled into thin sheets

1 tablespoon olive oil

3 cups (24 fl oz/750 ml) homemade or purchased meat sauce

1 cup (4 oz/125 g) grated Parmesan cheese

Pappardelle with Asparagus

Some markets sell asparagus trimmed down to the tender tips. If buying untrimmed asparagus, you will need to buy about double the weight indicated in this recipe. Use 2–5 inches (5–13 cm) of the tips and reserve the stalks for another use.

Bring a large pot three-fourths full of salted water to a boil over high heat. Add the asparagus tips and cook until tender, about 5 minutes; the timing will depend upon the thickness of the spears. Drain well, then slice on the diagonal into 3/4-inch (2-cm) lengths.

In a large sauté pan over medium heat, melt 2 tablespoons of the butter. Add the shallots and sauté until softened, about 2 minutes. Add the prosciutto and asparagus, season well with salt and pepper, and stir to coat with the seasonings. Remove from the heat and keep warm.

Again bring a large pot three-fourths full of salted water to a boil over high heat. Add the pasta, stir well, and cook until al dente (tender but firm to the bite), about 2 minutes for fresh pasta and 12 minutes or according to the package directions for dried.

Drain the pasta, reserving about 1/2 cup (4 fl oz/125 ml) of the cooking water. Return the pasta to the warm pot. Add the remaining 2 tablespoons butter, the Parmesan cheese, parsley, and asparagus mixture. Toss well. Add a little of the reserved cooking water if the pasta seems dry. Divide the sauced pasta among warmed dishes and serve at once.

Serves 4–6

1 1/2 lb (750 g) asparagus tips

4 tablespoons (2 oz/60 g) unsalted butter, at room temperature

1/4 cup (1 1/2 oz/45 g) minced shallots

2 oz (60 g) prosciutto, minced

Salt and freshly ground pepper

1 lb (500 g) fresh or dried pappardelle

1/2 cup (2 oz/60 g) grated Parmesan cheese

2 tablespoons minced fresh flat-leaf (Italian) parsley

Chicken Lasagna with Three Cheeses

Traditional lasagna is made a little spicy in this recipe. A hint of cayenne pepper brightens the fresh tomato sauce that is cooked with chicken and layered with pasta and a cooling mixture of ricotta, Parmesan, and mozzarella cheeses.

½ lb (250 g) dried lasagna noodles

1 teaspoon salt, plus more as needed

2 tablespoons olive oil

1 lb (500 g) ground (minced) chicken

1 large yellow onion, finely chopped

1 red bell pepper (capsicum), seeded and finely chopped

3 cloves garlic, minced

½ teaspoon cayenne pepper

3 lb (1.5 kg) tomatoes, peeled, seeded, and chopped

Freshly ground pepper

2 cups (1 lb/500 g) part-skim ricotta cheese

½ cup (2 oz/60 g) grated Parmesan or pecorino cheese

1 egg

½ cup (¾ oz/20 g) chopped fresh flat-leaf (Italian) parsley

½ lb (250 g) mozzarella cheese, shredded

Bring a large pot three-fourths full of water to a boil over high heat. Add the lasagna noodles and the 1 teaspoon salt, stir well, and cook until almost tender, about 8 minutes. Drain and rinse in cool water. Lay the noodles flat on a kitchen towel and set aside.

Preheat the oven to 350°F (180°C). Oil a 7-by-11-inch (18-by-28-cm) baking dish.

In a frying pan over medium-high heat, warm the olive oil. Add the chicken and cook, stirring, until browned, about 6 minutes. Add the onion and bell pepper and sauté until softened, about 2 minutes. Stir in the garlic and cayenne pepper and sauté until the garlic is softened, about 20 seconds. Add the tomatoes, stir well, and bring to a boil. Reduce the heat to low and simmer until thickened, about 20 minutes. Season with salt and pepper to taste. Remove from the heat.

In a bowl, combine the ricotta, Parmesan cheese, and egg and mix well. Stir in the parsley. Line the bottom of the prepared baking dish with about one-fourth of the lasagna noodles, arranging them, in a single layer, and cutting them as needed to fit. Spread with one-third of the ricotta mixture, sprinkle with one-third of the mozzarella, and then spoon on one-fourth of the sauce. Repeat the layering two more times, using up all of the ricotta mixture and the mozzarella. Top with the remaining noodles and finally the remaining chicken sauce.

Cover the lasagna and bake until heated through and the sauce is bubbling, about 45 minutes. Remove from the oven and let stand for 10 minutes. Cut into squares and serve.

Serves 4–6

Spinach Cannelloni

Wash the spinach well and place in a frying pan. Cover and cook over medium heat until wilted, about 3 minutes. Let cool and chop finely. In a bowl, combine the spinach, ricotta, mozzarella, egg, half of the garlic, and the minced basil. Season with salt and pepper to taste. Cover and refrigerate until needed.

Dust 3 baking sheets with semolina flour. Cut the pasta into 6-inch (15-cm) squares. Transfer the squares to the baking sheets and cover with kitchen towels.

Melt the butter in a saucepan over medium heat. Whisk in the flour. Cook, whisking constantly, for 1 minute. Add the milk and bring to a simmer, whisking constantly. Add the bay leaf and thyme, and season with nutmeg, salt, and pepper to taste. Cook gently, whisking often, for about 20 minutes. Press the sauce through a coarse-mesh sieve into a bowl.

In a sauté pan over medium heat, warm 2 tablespoons of the olive oil. Add the remaining garlic and red pepper flakes and sauté for 1 minute. Add the tomatoes and salt to taste. Simmer, uncovered, about 15 minutes. Pass the sauce through a food mill. Return to the sauté pan with the basil leaves and simmer for 5 minutes.

Preheat the oven to 400°F (200°C). Butter a 9-by-13-inch (23-by-33-cm) baking dish. Fill a large bowl with ice water and add the remaining 1 tablespoon olive oil. Bring a large pot three-fourths full of salted water to a boil over high heat. Cook the pasta squares, 2 sheets at a time, for 10 seconds only. Transfer to the ice water and unfurl the squares in the water, then lay flat on a damp kitchen towel and pat dry.

Spread a scant 1/4 cup (2 oz/60 g) of the spinach filling on each pasta square. Roll into a log, then place in the prepared dish. Top with the white sauce, then with the tomato sauce. Sprinkle with the Parmesan cheese. Bake, uncovered, until bubbling hot, about 20 minutes. Serve at once.

Serves 4–6

14–16 oz (440–500 g) fresh spinach leaves, stemmed

1/2 lb (250 g) whole-milk ricotta cheese

1/2 lb (250 g) whole-milk mozzarella cheese, shredded

1 egg

4 cloves garlic, minced

1 tablespoon minced fresh basil, plus 8 basil leaves, torn into pieces

Salt and freshly ground pepper

Semolina flour for dusting

3/4 lb (375 g) Fresh Spinach Pasta (page 290)

1 1/2 tablespoons unsalted butter

1 1/2 tablespoons unbleached all-purpose (plain) flour

1 cup (8 fl oz/250 ml) milk

1 bay leaf

1 fresh thyme sprig

Freshly grated nutmeg to taste

3 tablespoons olive oil

Pinch of red pepper flakes

1 can (14 1/2 oz/455 g) whole plum (Roma) tomatoes, chopped

1/2 cup (2 oz/60 g) grated Parmesan cheese

Pizzettas with Spring Herb Pesto

FOR THE SEMOLINA DOUGH:

1 package (2½ teaspoons) active dry yeast

2 tablespoons sugar

1½ cups (12 fl oz/375 ml) warm water (115°F/46°C)

3½ cups (17½ oz/545 g) all–purpose (plain) flour

½ cup (2½ oz/75 g) semolina flour

1 tablespoon salt

3 tablespoons olive oil

FOR THE PESTO:

¼ cup (1¼ oz/37 g) slivered blanched almonds

1 clove garlic

¼ cup (¼ oz/7 g) *each* fresh chervil leaves and flat–leaf (Italian) parsley leaves

¼ cup (¼ oz/7 g) snipped fresh chives

¼ cup (2 fl oz/60 ml) extra–virgin olive oil

¼ cup (1 oz/30 g) grated Parmesan cheese

¼ lb (125 g) part–skim mozzarella cheese, shredded

3 tomatoes, thinly sliced

To make the dough, in a small bowl, dissolve the yeast and sugar in the warm water; let stand until bubbles rise, about 5 minutes.

In a large bowl, combine the all-purpose flour, semolina flour, and salt. Stir in the yeast mixture and olive oil until a dough forms. Turn out the dough onto a lightly floured work surface and knead until smooth, 5–8 minutes. Form into a ball and place in a lightly oiled bowl, turning to coat all sides. Cover with plastic wrap and let rise for 30 minutes.

Turn out the dough onto a lightly floured work surface, press flat, and divide into 8 equal portions. Form each portion into a ball and place on a lightly oiled baking sheet. Cover and let rise until almost doubled in bulk, about 45 minutes.

Meanwhile, make the pesto: Preheat the oven to 350°F (180°C). Spread the almonds on a baking sheet and toast until lightly browned, 5–7 minutes, let cool. With a food processor running, drop in the garlic clove, then add the chervil, parsley, chives, and toasted almonds and process to a grainy texture. Again with the food processor running, add the olive oil in a slow stream until combined. Pour into a bowl and fold in the Parmesan cheese. Set aside.

Raise the oven temperature to 450°F (230°C). Place a pizza stone in the oven to preheat or oil another baking sheet. On the lightly floured work surface, roll out each ball of dough into a round 6 inches (15 cm) in diameter. Leaving a ½-inch (12-mm) border, spread 1 tablespoon of the pesto over each round. Sprinkle a little mozzarella cheese over each round, then arrange the tomato slices on top.

Baking in 2 batches, transfer the pizzettas to the prepared baking sheet or pizza stone and bake until the dough is lightly browned and the cheese is melted, about 10 minutes. Serve at once.

Makes eight 6-inch (15-cm) pizzas; serves 4

Pasta with Chicken Meatballs

Flavored with prosciutto and punctuated with pine nuts, these light meatballs are delicious when served over a robust-shaped pasta such as penne or ziti. You can also serve the meatballs as an appetizer and reserve the sauce for tossing the pasta.

Preheat the broiler (grill). Cut the bell pepper in half lengthwise and remove the stem and seeds. Place the pepper, cut sides down, on a baking sheet. Broil (grill) until the skin blackens and blisters. Remove from the broiler, cover the pepper loosely with aluminum foil, let cool for 10 minutes, then peel away the skin. Transfer to a blender or food processor and purée until smooth. Set aside.

In a bowl, combine the chicken and half of the onion. Add the prosciutto, garlic, oregano, basil, rosemary, and egg and mix well with your hands. Add enough of the bread crumbs to bind the mixture. Mix in the parsley and toasted pine nuts, and season with salt and pepper. Pinch off walnut-sized pieces and roll into balls.

In a frying pan over medium-high heat, warm the olive oil. Add the meatballs in batches and cook, turning as needed, until well browned on all sides, about 5 minutes. Transfer to a plate. Pour off all but 1 tablespoon of the fat from the pan and place over medium-high heat. Add the remaining onion and sauté until softened, about 2 minutes. Return the meatballs to the pan and add the Classic Tomato Sauce and red pepper purée. Bring to a boil, reduce the heat to medium-low, cover, and simmer until the meatballs are cooked through, about 20 minutes.

Meanwhile, bring a large pot three-fourths full of salted water to a boil over high heat. Add the pasta, stir well, and cook until al dente, 10–12 minutes or according to the package directions. Drain and place in a warmed serving bowl. Ladle the meatballs and sauce over the pasta and serve. Pass the Parmesan cheese at the table.

Serves 4

1 red bell pepper (capsicum)

1½ lb (750 g) ground (minced) chicken

1 yellow onion, finely chopped

2 oz (60 g) prosciutto, minced

2 cloves garlic, minced

2 teaspoons finely chopped fresh oregano

2 teaspoons finely chopped fresh basil

2 teaspoons finely chopped fresh rosemary

1 egg

⅓–½ cup (1½–2 oz/45–60 g) fine dried bread crumbs

⅓ cup (½ oz/15 g) chopped fresh flat-leaf (Italian) parsley

¼ cup (1½ oz/45 g) pine nuts, toasted

Salt and freshly ground pepper

2 tablespoons olive oil

Classic Tomato Sauce (page 290)

¾ lb (375 g) penne or ziti

½ cup (2 oz/60 g) grated Parmesan cheese

Main Dishes

Pan-Seared Halibut with Baby Vegetables

This recipe calls for baby turnips, carrots, and fennel, which are more mild in flavor and more delicate in texture than when the vegetables are fully mature. Other firm-fleshed white fish such as sea bass or snapper can be substituted for the halibut.

12 small, young turnips, with greens intact

12 baby carrots

1 baby fennel bulb

1 tablespoon unsalted butter

1 teaspoon salt

1/2 teaspoon freshly ground pepper

1/3 cup (3 fl oz/80 ml) dry white wine

4 halibut steaks or fillets, about 5 oz (155 g) each and 1/2 inch (12 mm) thick

Trim the turnips, cutting off the green tops. Choose the nicest, smallest leaves and reserve them; discard the rest. Cut the turnips into slices about $^1/_8$ inch (3 mm) thick. Trim the carrots and cut in half lengthwise. Cut off the stems, feathery tops, and bruised outer stalks from the fennel bulb. Cut the bulb crosswise into slices about $^1/_8$ inch (3 mm) thick.

In a frying pan over medium-high heat, melt $^1/_2$ tablespoon of the butter. When it foams, add the turnips, fennel, and carrots and sauté until tender, 2–3 minutes. Sprinkle with $^1/_2$ teaspoon of the salt and $^1/_4$ teaspoon of the pepper and continue to cook, stirring occasionally, until lightly browned, 1–2 minutes longer. Reserve 4 raw attractive turnip leaves for garnish and add the rest to the pan along with the white wine. Reduce the heat to low, cover, and cook until the vegetables are tender, about 2 minutes longer. Keep warm.

In a large frying pan over medium-high heat, melt the remaining $^1/_2$ tablespoon butter. When it foams, add the fish, sprinkle with the remaining $^1/_2$ teaspoon salt and $^1/_4$ teaspoon pepper, and cook until browned on the underside, 1–2 minutes. Turn over the fish and continue to cook until browned on the second side and opaque throughout, 2–3 minutes longer.

To serve, spoon one-fourth of the vegetable mixture onto each warmed individual plate. Place a piece of fish alongside, garnish with a reserved turnip leaf, and serve at once.

Serves 4

Asian Tuna Burgers with Wasabi Mayonnaise

Asian flavors give this classy tuna burger a sprightly edge. To lighten the sandwich further, slice each bagel horizontally into thirds instead of halves, reserving the center slice for another use. The tuna patty is also delicious served on a bed of greens.

Using a vegetable peeler, shave off lengthwise slices of the cucumber into thin ribbons. Set aside. In a bowl, lightly mix together the tuna, green onions, fresh ginger, and egg white. Season with salt and pepper. Using your hands, shape the tuna mixture into 4 patties, each 4 inches (10 cm) in diameter.

In a small bowl, whisk together the mayonnaise, pickled ginger, and wasabi. Spread the mayonnaise mixture onto the cut sides of the bagels.

Heat a large nonstick frying pan over medium-high heat. Coat the pan with nonstick cooking spray. Add the tuna patties to the pan and cook until golden on the first side, about 2 minutes. Turn over the patties and continue to cook until golden on the second side and medium-rare in the center, about 2 minutes longer.

Using a spatula, place a patty on the bottom slice of each bagel. Top with the cucumber ribbons and some of the sprouts, dividing them evenly. Divide the remaining sprouts among the bagel tops, sticking them into the holes. Place atop the burgers and serve at once.

Serves 4

1 small English (hothouse) cucumber

1 lb (500 g) ahi tuna fillet, chopped

3 green (spring) onions, chopped

2 tablespoons peeled and minced fresh ginger

1 extra-large egg white

Salt and freshly ground pepper

3 tablespoons fat-free mayonnaise

3 tablespoons chopped pickled ginger

1 1/2 teaspoons prepared wasabi

4 sesame bagels, halved and toasted

1 package (3 1/2 oz/105 g) daikon sprouts

Rutabaga, Squash, and Mushroom Ragout

A ragout is simply a well-seasoned stew with a thick sauce. Simmered slowly, this autumn dish with deep, rich flavors is at once satisfying and healthy. Serve this combination over couscous or brown rice.

3 tablespoons extra-virgin olive oil

1 large red onion, diced

2 cups (16 fl oz/500 ml) Vegetable Stock (page 289) or broth

1 cup (8 fl oz/250 ml) carrot juice

2 rutabagas, peeled and finely diced

1 winter squash, about 1 lb (500 g), peeled, seeded, and diced

1 butternut squash, about 1 lb (500 g), peeled and diced

1 lb (500 g) fresh button mushrooms, brushed clean, stemmed and quartered

1 cup (6 oz/185 g) pitted prunes, coarsely chopped

$^1/_2$ teaspoon dried thyme

$^1/_2$ teaspoon dried marjoram

Salt and freshly ground pepper

2 tablespoons minced fresh flat-leaf (Italian) parsley

In a heavy saucepan over medium heat, warm the olive oil. Add the onion and sauté until softened, about 5 minutes. Add the stock and carrot juice, raise the heat to high, and bring to a boil. Add the rutabagas and squashes, reduce the heat to medium-low, and simmer, uncovered, for 30 minutes.

Add the mushrooms, prunes, thyme, and marjoram to the pan and continue to cook until all the vegetables are tender, 15–20 minutes longer. Season to taste with salt and pepper.

To serve, ladle the ragout into warmed bowls and sprinkle with the parsley. Serve immediately.

Serves 6

Tofu and Mixed Vegetable Curry

In winter months, when fresh produce is scarce, you can still put an exciting meal on the table with just a few simple ingredients. Serve this curry over steamed rice, and garnish with toasted flaked coconut.

In a small dry frying pan over medium heat, toast the coconut, stirring occasionally, until golden brown, about 5 minutes. Transfer to a plate and set aside.

In a large saucepan over medium heat, warm the vegetable oil. Add the onions and sauté until softened, 4–6 minutes. Add the carrot and garlic and sauté until softened, 2–3 minutes longer.

Add the coconut milk and curry powder, raise the heat to medium-high, and bring to a boil. Add the broccoli, cauliflower, and tofu and reduce the heat to medium-low. Simmer, uncovered, until the vegetables are tender, 5–7 minutes. Season with salt, to taste.

Transfer the vegetable-tofu mixture to a warmed serving dish and serve at once.

Serves 6

3 tablespoons shredded unsweetened coconut

3 tablespoons vegetable oil

2 yellow onions, sliced

1 carrot, peeled and grated

2 cloves garlic, minced

2 cups (16 fl oz/500 ml) unsweetened coconut milk

2 tablespoons curry powder

2 cups (4 oz/125 g) broccoli florets

1 cup (2 oz/60 g) cauliflower florets

6 oz (185 g) firm tofu, cut into 1/2-inch (12-mm) cubes

Salt

Shrimp and Tomatoes in Chile Sauce

In Malaysia, this dish is called *udang* ("shrimp") *goreng* ("fried"). Cooking the dish is as simple as its translation, but the final result has a complex layering of flavor: a refreshing citrus base accentuated with strong savory notes and a spicy heat.

2 candlenuts or blanched almonds

3 shallots, quartered

2 large jalapeño chiles, seeded and quartered

2 cloves garlic, halved

1 teaspoon shrimp paste or anchovy paste

3 tablespoons vegetable oil

1 yellow onion, cut into wedges 1/4 inch (2 cm) wide

3/4 lb (375 g) large shrimp (prawns), peeled and deveined with tails intact, patted dry

1 stalk lemongrass, center and white part only, chopped

1 tablespoon sugar

1/2 teaspoon salt

2 firm tomatoes, cut into wedges 1/2 inch (12 mm) wide

2–3 tablespoons lime juice

Place the nuts in a small bowl, cover with water, and let stand until moist, about 5 minutes. Drain. In a blender, combine the soaked nuts, shallots, chiles, garlic, shrimp paste, and just enough water to facilitate blending, up to 2 tablespoons. Process until a smooth paste forms. Set aside.

Warm a wok or frying pan over medium-high heat. Add 1 tablespoon of the oil. When hot, add the onion and toss and stir until translucent, about 1 minute. Raise the heat to high, add the shrimp, and toss and stir until they turn bright orange, about 2 minutes. Transfer to a plate.

Return the wok to medium-high heat and add the remaining 2 tablespoons oil. When hot, add the nut-spice paste and the lemongrass and toss and stir until fragrant and blended with the oil, 3–4 minutes. Continue to cook, stirring frequently, until the oil separates from the spice paste, 5–8 minutes. Add the sugar and salt, raise the heat to high, and add the shrimp mixture and the tomatoes. Toss and stir until heated through, about 30 seconds.

Drizzle with the lime juice to taste and serve hot.

Serves 4–6

Scallops in Green Curry Sauce

For this Thai-style curry, scallops are seared and then immersed in a creamy sauce. Serve this hearty curry with steamed rice and a vegetable side dish such as Stir-fried Pea Shoots with Garlic (page 190).

Open the can of coconut milk without shaking it, scrape $1/3$ cup (3 fl oz/80 ml) of the thick cream from the top, place it in a wide saucepan. Add the green curry paste and cook and cook over medium-high heat, stirring frequently, until beads of oil appear in the paste, about 5 minutes. Add the fish sauce, sugar, 8 lime leaves, and the remaining coconut milk and cook, uncovered, stirring constantly, until the mixture is the consistency of a cream sauce, about 5 minutes. Taste and adjust the seasonings. Remove from the heat and set aside.

Bring a saucepan three-fourths full of water to a boil over high heat. Add the squash and zucchini and blanch until tender-crisp, 2–3 minutes. Drain and rinse under running cold water to stop the cooking.

Warm a wide, heavy frying pan over medium-high heat. Add $1/2$ teaspoon of the oil and tilt the pan to spread the oil evenly over the bottom. Remove any excess oil with paper towels. When the oil is nearly smoking, place the scallops in the pan in a single layer, and cook, turning once, until seared, about 1 minute on each side. Season to taste with salt and pepper, transfer to a plate, and cover loosely. Return the pan to medium-high heat and warm the remaining $1 1/2$ teaspoons oil. Add the eggplant chunks and cook, stirring constantly, until they begins to soften and are well browned at the edges, 3–5 minutes. Add the blanched squash and zucchini, the sauce, and the basil and cook until the basil wilts and the sauce is heated through, about 30 seconds. Add the scallops and stir gently to coat with the sauce.

Serve hot, garnished with the slivered lime leaves.

Serves 4

1 can (13$1/2$ fl oz/425 ml) unsweetened coconut milk

2 tablespoons Thai green curry paste

1 tablespoon Thai fish sauce

1 teaspoon palm sugar or firmly packed dark brown sugar

8 fresh or frozen kaffir lime leaves, plus 3 leaves, finely slivered, for garnish

1 yellow crookneck squash, cut into irregular 3/4-inch (2-cm) chunks

1 small zucchini (courgette), cut into irregular 3/4-inch (2-cm) chunks

2 teaspoons vegetable oil

1 lb (500 g) large sea scallops, muscle removed

Salt and freshly ground pepper

2 Asian eggplants (slender aubergines), cut into irregular 3/4-inch (2-cm) chunks

1/2 cup (1/2 oz/15 g) Thai basil or sweet basil leaves

Veal Piccata

Veal scallops, or cutlets, are thin, tender slices of veal cut from the loin or leg. They are best sautéed or pan-fried. Here they are enhanced with an easy pan sauce of capers, lemon, and parsley.

1¹/₂ lb (750 g) veal scallops (about 8 total), about ¹/₂ inch (12 mm) thick

1 cup (5 oz/155 g) all-purpose (plain) flour

Salt and freshly ground pepper

4 tablespoons (2 oz/60 g) unsalted butter

2 tablespoons olive oil

1 cup (8 fl oz/250 ml) Chicken Stock (page 288) or broth

3 tablespoons fresh lemon juice

¹/₄ cup (2 oz/60 g) capers, rinsed (optional)

2 tablespoons chopped fresh flat-leaf (Italian) parsley

One at a time, place the veal scallops between 2 sheets of plastic wrap and gently pound with a meat pounder until about ¹/₄ inch (6 mm) thick.

Spread the flour on a plate and season with salt and pepper. One at a time, dip the pounded veal scallops in the seasoned flour, coating evenly, and then shake off the excess. In a sauté pan large enough to accommodate all the veal slices in a single layer (or 2 pans), melt 2 tablespoons of the butter with the olive oil over medium-high heat. Add the veal scallops and sauté, turning once, until golden, 3–4 minutes per side. Transfer to a warmed platter or warmed individual plates and keep warm.

Discard any burnt butter and oil and return the pan to high heat. Pour in the stock and deglaze the pan, stirring with a wooden spoon to scrape up any browned bits from the pan bottom. Boil until reduced by half, 8–10 minutes. Stir in the lemon juice, capers (if using), and the remaining 2 tablespoons butter just until the butter melts.

Pour the sauce over the veal scallops and sprinkle with the parsley. Serve at once.

Serves 4

Braised Tuna with Eggplant, Tomato, and Olives

The key to preparing fresh tuna, which is very lean, is not to overcook it. Add the fillets to a very hot pan and quickly sear each side. For the best results, remove from the heat while it is still pink in the center.

In a frying pan over medium-high heat, warm 2 teaspoons of the olive oil. Add the eggplant, season with salt to taste, and sauté until lightly browned, about 3 minutes. Remove from the heat, add the garlic, and stir for about 15 seconds. Return to the heat and add the tomatoes, basil, and olives. Bring to a simmer, cover, and adjust the heat to maintain a gentle simmer. Cook until the eggplant is just tender, about 5 minutes, adding a little water if the mixture gets too thick.

Season the tuna with salt and pepper, add to the frying pan, and drizzle with the remaining 1 teaspoon olive oil. Cover and simmer gently for 2 minutes, then turn the tuna over, cover, and cook until it just flakes with a fork, about 1 1/2 minutes longer. It should still be pink in the center; do not overcook it or it will be dry.

Using a spatula, transfer the tuna to warmed individual plates. If the sauce is a little thin, continue to cook over medium-high heat until reduced to the desired consistency. Spoon the sauce over and around the tuna. Serve at once.

Serves 4

1 tablespoon olive oil

4 Asian eggplants (slender aubergines), each about 3 oz (90 g), unpeeled, cut into 1/2-inch (12-mm) dice

Salt

3 small clove garlic, minced

1 cup (6 oz/185 g) grated plum (Roma) tomatoes

8 fresh basil leaves, torn into small pieces

1/2 cup (2 1/2 oz/75 g) Niçoise olives, pitted and coarsely chopped

4 tuna fillets, about 6 oz (185 g), each no more than 1/2 inch (12 mm) thick

Freshly ground pepper

Ancho Chile Fajitas

Fajitas make a quick-and-easy midweek dinner. Provide Pico de gallo, sour cream, cilantro (coriander) leaves and lime wedges as condiments. Let your guests garnish and wrap their own fajitas.

In a saucepan, bring 2 cups (16 fl oz/500 ml) water to a boil. Remove from the heat and add the ancho chiles. Cover and let stand off the heat until the chiles are soft, about 15 minutes. Using tongs, remove the chiles from the soaking water; reserve the liquid. When cool enough to handle, slit the chiles lengthwise and seed them. Discard the stems and seeds. Place the ancho chiles, garlic, and 3 tablespoons of the soaking liquid in a blender and process until a smooth puree forms. Set aside.

Place the flank steak in a shallow, nonaluminum bowl. Add $1/3$ cup (3 fl oz/80 ml) of the ancho purée and turn the steak to coat both sides. Cover the bowl and refrigerate for at least 6 hours or up to overnight. Reserve the remaining purée in a separate covered bowl in the refrigerator.

In a large nonstick frying pan over medium heat, warm 1 tablespoon of the olive oil. Add the Anaheim chiles, bell peppers, onion, cumin, and salt and pepper to taste and sauté until soft, about 25 minutes. Remove from the heat and keep warm.

Meanwhile, warm the remaining 1 tablespoon olive oil in another nonstick frying pan over medium heat. Season the steak lightly with salt and add to the pan. Cook until the meat is well browned on the first side, about 5 minutes. Turn and continue to cook until medium-rare in the center, about 4 minutes longer. Transfer the steak to a cutting board and let rest for 4–5 minutes. To serve, thinly slice the steak across the grain and place in a bowl. Add 3 tablespoons of the reserved ancho purée and mix well. Transfer the vegetables and the steak to a warmed platter. Serve with the tortillas.

Serves 4

3 ancho chiles

8 cloves garlic

1 lb (500 g) beef flank steak, trimmed of excess fat

2 tablespoons olive oil

4 large Anaheim chiles, sliced crosswise

2 red bell peppers (capsicums), seeded and sliced

1 red onion, sliced

1 tablespoon ground cumin

Salt and freshly ground pepper

8 flour tortillas, each 6 inches (15 cm) in diameter, heated

Chicken in Coconut Milk

Coconut milk provides a cool, creamy balance to the heat of the minced chile in this Southeast Asian-inspired dish. Chicken thighs stand up to this preparation better than breasts, as they remain more succulent during simmering.

In a heavy frying pan over high heat, warm the oil until very hot. Add the chicken and sauté, turning once, until browned, about 3 minutes on each side. Season to taste with salt and pepper.

Reduce the heat to medium and add the shallot and chile. Standing back from the pan so you don't inhale the fumes from the chile, sauté until softened, about 1 minute. Stir in the coconut milk, fish sauce (if using), and lime juice. Bring to a boil, reduce the heat to low, and simmer, uncovered, turning the chicken occasionally, until the chicken is opaque throughout and the sauce has thickened, about 20 minutes.

Using tongs, transfer the chicken thighs to a warmed serving dish or warmed individual plates. Spoon the sauce over the top. Garnish with the lime zest and serve.

Serves 4

2 tablespoons canola or safflower oil

8 chicken thighs, about 6 oz (185 g) each, skinned

Salt and freshly ground pepper

1 shallot, finely chopped

1 red or green Thai chile, seeded and minced

1½ cups (12 fl oz/375 ml) unsweetened coconut milk

1 teaspoon fish sauce (optional)

Juice and zest of 1 lime

Italian Sausage with Peperonata

For an authentic taste, look for a sausage seasoned with fennel seeds. If you can't find one, add a pinch of fennel seeds to the tomato-and-pepper mixture, or peperonata. Serve spooned over soft polenta.

¼ cup olive oil

1 yellow onion, thinly sliced

3 cloves garlic, minced

1 cup (6 oz/185 g) grated plum (Roma) tomatoes

3 red bell peppers (capsicums), seeded and thinly sliced lengthwise

8 fresh basil leaves, torn into small pieces

Salt and freshly ground pepper

1 lb (500g) Italian-style pork, turkey, or chicken sausage links

In a small frying pan over medium-low heat, warm 2 tablespoons of the olive oil. Add the onion and garlic and sauté until softened, about 5 minutes. Add the tomatoes and sauté for about 5 minutes to develop the flavors. Add the bell peppers, basil, and salt and pepper to taste and stir well. Add ¼ cup water, cover, and simmer gently until the peppers are tender, 25–30 minutes, adding a little more water if the mixture looks too dry. Transfer to a bowl.

Rinse the frying pan and place over medium heat. Add the remaining 2 tablespoons olive oil. Prick the sausages in 3 or 4 places with a knife, add them to the frying pan, and cook until browned on all sides and no longer pink inside, about 10 minutes. Pierce with a knife to check for doneness. Transfer to a cutting board. Pour off any fat in the frying pan, add the pepper mixture, and reheat gently.

Cut the sausage on the diagonal into slices ½ inch (12 mm) thick. Transfer the tomato-pepper mixture to warmed dinner plates and top with the sausage. Serve at once.

Serves 4

Italian Sausage Sandwich with Sautéed Onions and Peppers

Make this hearty sandwich during summer and autumn when farmers' markets are ablaze with different colors and varieties of sweet peppers. Serve with a tossed green salad for a satisfying lunch or dinner.

Cut each sausage in half lengthwise. In a large frying pan over medium heat, fry the sausages, turning once, until cooked through, 4–5 minutes on each side. Remove from the heat and keep warm.

In a frying pan over medium-high heat, warm the oil. When the oil is hot, add the onions and cook, scraping and turning often, until limp and slightly browned, 7–8 minutes. Transfer to a bowl and keep warm.

Add the the green, red, and orange peppers to the pan and cook the same way until they are limp and browned on the edges, about 10 minutes. Add the balsamic vinegar and deglaze the pan, stirring to scrape up any browned bits from the pan bottom, 1–2 minutes longer.

To make the sandwiches, lightly spread the cut sides of the toasted rolls with the mustard. Divide the onions, the pepper mixture, and the sausage halves evenly among the roll bottoms, allowing 3 pieces of sausage for each sandwich.

Serve the sandwiches open-faced.

Serves 4

6 hot or sweet Italian sausages, about 1½ lb (750 g) total weight

2 tablespoons olive oil

2 large red onions, thinly sliced

4 long, green Italian sweet peppers (capsicums), seeded and cut into thin rounds

2 red bell peppers (capsicums), seeded and cut lengthwise into strips ¼ inch (6 mm) wide

1 orange bell pepper (capsicum), seeded and cut lengthwise into strips ¼ inch (6 mm) wide

2 tablespoons balsamic vinegar

4 sourdough or other sandwich rolls, split and toasted

2 tablespoons Dijon mustard

Chicken Pot Pie with Cornmeal Crust

Preheat the oven to 375°F (190°C).

Prepare the vegetables: Chop the green onions; seed and chop the bell pepper; and mince the garlic. In a frying pan over medium-high heat, warm the 2 tablespoons oil. Add the green onions and bell pepper and sauté until softened, about 3 minutes. Add the garlic and sauté until softened, about 20 seconds longer. Remove from the heat and stir in the chicken, green and serrano chiles, cilantro, oregano, rice, and stock. Seed and chop the tomatoes and add them to the chicken-rice mixture. Season to taste with salt and pepper. Pour into a shallow, 6-cup (48-fl oz/1.5-l) baking dish.

In a bowl, stir together the cornmeal, flour, baking powder, chili powder, and ¹⁄₂ teaspoon salt until well mixed. Stir in the jack cheese.

In another bowl, using a whisk, beat the egg until blended, then beat in the milk and the ¹⁄₃ cup (3 fl oz/80 ml) oil until well combined. Pour the liquid mixture into the flour mixture and stir to mix well. Spoon evenly over the chicken-rice mixture in the dish.

Bake until the crust is puffed and golden brown and the chicken filling is bubbling, 25–30 minutes. Serve hot directly from the dish.

Serves 4–6

6 green (spring) onions

1 green bell pepper (capsicum)

2 cloves garlic

2 tablespoons canola oil, plus ¹⁄₃ cup (3 fl oz/80 ml)

1¹⁄₂ lb (750 g) cooked chicken meat, cubed

1 can (3¹⁄₂ oz/105 g) chopped green chiles, drained

1 serrano chile, seeded and minced

¹⁄₂ cup (¹⁄₂ oz/15 g) fresh cilantro (fresh coriander) leaves

1 tablespoon chopped fresh oregano

1 cup (5 oz/155 g) cooked white rice

¹⁄₂ cup (4 fl oz/125 ml) Chicken Stock (page 288) or broth

4 plum (Roma) tomatoes

Salt and freshly ground pepper

1 cup (5 oz/155 g) *each* finely ground yellow cornmeal and all-purpose (plain) flour

1 tablespoon baking powder

1 teaspoon chili powder

¹⁄₂ cup (2 oz/60 g) Monterey jack cheese, shredded

1 egg

1 cup (8 fl oz/250 ml) whole milk

Chicken, Sausage, and Seafood Paella

4 *each* small chicken thighs and breast halves

2¹/₂ tablespoons finely minced garlic

1¹/₂ tablespoons dried oregano

2 teaspoons coarsely ground pepper

1 teaspoon salt

3 tablespoons red wine vinegar

5 tablespoons (2¹/₂ fl oz/75 ml) extra-virgin olive oil

¹/₂ teaspoon saffron threads

¹/₄ cup (2 fl oz/60 ml) dry white wine

6 oz (185 g) Spanish chorizo

6 tablespoons (3 fl oz/90 ml) olive oil

2 yellow onions, chopped

2–3 cups (12–18 oz/375–560 g) canned tomatoes

1¹/₂ cups (10¹/₂ oz/330 g) short-grain white rice

4 cups (32 fl oz/1 l) Chicken Stock (page 288) or broth

16 shrimp (prawns), peeled and deveined

1 cup (5 oz/155 g) frozen petite peas, thawed

24 clams or mussels, debearded and scrubbed

Rinse the chicken pieces and pat dry. In a small bowl, stir together 1¹/₂ tablespoons of the garlic, the oregano, pepper, and salt. Stir in the vinegar. Stir in the extra-virgin olive oil to form a paste. Rub the paste on the chicken and place in a nonreactive container. Cover and refrigerate overnight.

Crumble the saffron into a small saucepan, add the wine, and bring to a simmer. Remove from the heat and let steep for 10 minutes. In a frying pan over medium-high heat, sauté the chorizo until golden brown, about 5 minutes. Cut the chorizo into 1-inch (2.5-cm) chunks and set aside.

In a large frying pan over high heat, warm about 3 tablespoons of the olive oil. Add the marinated chicken pieces and brown on all sides, about 10 minutes. Using tongs, transfer to a plate. Wipe out the pan. Add the remaining 2 tablespoons oil and place over medium heat. Add the onions and sauté until soft, about 10 minutes. Add the tomatoes and remaining 1 tablespoon garlic and cook, stirring occasionally, about 5 minutes. Add the rice and stir until opaque, about 3 minutes. Raise the heat to high, add the stock, saffron and wine. Bring to a boil, reduce the heat to low, and simmer, uncovered, until the rice is half cooked, about 10 minutes. Return the chicken to the pan and cook until most of the liquid has been absorbed and the chicken is cooked through, about 10 minutes longer. Stir in the shrimp, chorizo, and peas during the final 5–8 minutes of cooking; the shrimp will be opaque when ready.

Meanwhile, in a wide saucepan, pour water to a depth of 1 inch (2.5 cm). Add the clams or mussels, discarding any that do not close to the touch, cover, and place over medium-high heat. Steam, shaking the pan occasionally, until the shellfish open, 3–5 minutes. Discard any that failed to open. Stir the clams or mussels and their pan juices into the paella. Let stand for 10 minutes before serving.

Serves 4

Fried Chicken with Herbs

An updated version of a traditional Sunday favorite, this fried chicken is enlivened with herbs. First browned in oil and then finished in a hot oven, this chicken is less messy, but just as delicious as the traditional deep-fried dish.

Place the chicken pieces in a bowl with 1 cup (8 fl oz/250 ml) of the buttermilk. Cover and refrigerate for at least 1 hour or up to 18 hours.

Preheat the oven to 400°F (200°C). In a shallow bowl, beat the egg until blended, then beat in the remaining 1/2 cup (4 fl oz/125 ml) buttermilk. On a plate, mix together the flour, bread crumbs, garlic, basil, marjoram, paprika, salt, and pepper.

Using tongs, lift the chicken pieces from the buttermilk, one at a time, and dip first into the flour mixture, coating evenly, and then into the egg mixture. Dip each piece again into the flour mixture and set aside on a baking sheet. When all the chicken pieces are coated, refrigerate them for 15 minutes while the oil heats.

In a deep frying pan over high heat, pour in oil to a depth of 1 inch (2.5 cm). Heat the oil until it reaches 350°F (180°C) on a deep-frying thermometer, or until the corner of a piece of chicken dipped into the hot oil sizzles immediately upon contact. Working in batches, fry the chicken pieces, turning as needed, until well browned on all sides, about 10 minutes total. Do not crowd the pan. As soon as the pieces are browned, transfer them to a clean baking sheet.

When all of the pieces are browned, place them in the oven and bake until opaque throughout and the juices run clear, 20–30 minutes. Breasts will take a shorter amount of time, while thighs and drumsticks will take longer. As the pieces are done, transfer them to a plate. Arrange all the pieces on a warmed serving platter and serve warm or at room temperature, garnished with the chopped parsley.

Serves 4

2 chickens, about 2 1/2 lb (1.25 kg), cut into 8 pieces each

1 1/2 cups (12 fl oz/375 ml) buttermilk

1 egg

3/4 cup (4 oz/125 g) all-purpose (plain) flour

3/4 cup (3 oz/90 g) fine dried bread crumbs

2 cloves garlic, minced

1 tablespoon finely chopped fresh basil

1 tablespoon finely chopped fresh marjoram

1 teaspoon paprika

1 teaspoon salt

1/2 teaspoon freshly ground pepper

Canola oil for frying

2 tablespoons chopped fresh flat-leaf (Italian) parsley

Poached Salmon with Cucumber Raita

Raita is a traditional Indian salad of vegetables and yogurt, served as a cooling condiment alongside curries. To round out an Indian-themed meal, accompany the fish with basmati rice tossed with corn, peas, diced tomatoes, and mint.

Fill a shallow, wide sauté pan three-fourths full of water and add 1 teaspoon of the curry powder. Bring to a boil over high heat. Add the salmon, turn off the heat, and let stand for 8 minutes. Turn and continue to let stand until the salmon is opaque throughout, about 5 minutes longer. Using a slotted spatula, transfer the salmon fillets to individual plates. Cover and chill for 3–6 hours.

Meanwhile, in a small bowl, stir together the remaining 1 teaspoon curry powder, the cucumber, red onion, yogurt, cilantro, chopped mint, and cumin. Season to taste with salt and pepper. Cover and refrigerate until serving.

To serve, spoon the raita over the salmon fillets, dividing it evenly. Garnish with the mint sprigs.

Serves 6

2 teaspoons curry powder

6 salmon fillets, about 5 oz (155 g) each

1 large cucumber, peeled, seeded, and chopped

1 cup (4 oz/125 g) chopped red onion

1/2 cup (4 oz/125 g) plain nonfat yogurt

1/4 cup (1/3 oz/10 g) chopped fresh cilantro (fresh coriander)

3 tablespoons chopped fresh mint, plus sprigs for garnish

1 teaspoon ground cumin

Salt and freshly ground pepper

Turkey Burgers with Pepper-Corn Relish

Burgers made with ground turkey and seasoned with cumin, lime, and cayenne are lower in fat than traditional beef burgers. The piquant pepper-corn relish adds both flavor and color. Cook the burgers on an outdoor grill, if you like.

FOR THE RELISH:

1 teaspoon olive oil

1 cup (6 oz/185 g) corn kernels

1 red bell pepper (capsicum), seeded and chopped

6 tablespoons (2 oz/60 g) finely chopped red onion

1¼ teaspoons minced garlic

⅛ teaspoon salt

⅛ teaspoon freshly ground black pepper

1½ tablespoons fresh lime juice

1½ tablespoons chopped fresh cilantro (fresh coriander)

FOR THE BURGERS:

1 lb (500 g) ground (minced) turkey

2 teaspoons ground cumin

1½ teaspoons grated lime zest

1½ teaspoons fresh lime juice

¾ teaspoon salt

⅛ teaspoon cayenne pepper

8 thin slices pepper jack cheese

4 ciabatta rolls, split and lightly toasted

To make the relish, in a large, heavy frying pan over medium heat, warm the olive oil. When hot, add the corn and bell pepper and cook, stirring, constantly, for 5 minutes. Add the onion and garlic and cook, stirring, until the onion is softened, about 3 minutes. Stir in the salt and black pepper. Remove from the heat, transfer to a nonreactive bowl, and stir in the lime juice and cilantro. Taste and adjust the seasonings. Cover and let stand at room temperature for 1 hour. (The relish can be prepared 4–5 hours ahead, covered, and refrigerated. Bring to room temperature 30 minutes before using.)

Meanwhile, make the burgers: In a bowl, combine the turkey, cumin, lime zest and juice, salt, and cayenne. Mix well to blend. Divide the turkey mixture into 4 portions and shape each portion onto a patty ½ inch (12 mm) thick. Cover and refrigerate for at least 30 minutes or up to 5 hours.

When ready to serve, spray a large, heavy frying pan with nonstick cooking spray and place over medium heat. When hot, add the patties and cook, turning once, until cooked throughout, about 4 minutes per side. Place 2 slices of the cheese on each patty and cook until the cheese melts, about 1 minute longer.

Place the rolls on individual plates, cut sides up. Transfer the patties to the bottom halves of the rolls and top with the roll tops. Pass the relish at the table.

Serves 4

Seafood Curry with Coconut, Citrus, and Cucumber

In a small, dry frying pan over medium heat, toast the coriander and cumin, shaking the pan often, until fragrant, 2–3 minutes; set aside.

In a large saucepan over medium heat, warm the peanut oil. Add the onion and sauté until translucent, about 5 minutes. Add the ginger, garlic, lime zest, lemongrass, chile, and toasted spices and cook, stirring, until fragrant, 3–4 minutes. Add the coconut milk, broth, puréed cilantro, lime juice, and brown sugar. Bring to a boil, and immediately reduce the heat to low. Simmer for 5 minutes to blend the flavors. Season with salt and set aside.

Meanwhile, clean the squid: Working with 1 squid at a time, pull the head from the body. Cut the head from the tentacles above the eyes and discard the head. Squeeze the hard "beak" from the base of the tentacles. Set the tentacles aside. Remove the plasticlike quill from the body and discard; rinse the body well and peel off the speckled skin. Cut the body into rings 1 inch (2.5 cm) wide. Set aside.

Bring a saucepan three-fourths full of salted water to a boil. Meanwhile, cut the cucumbers lengthwise into quarters, scoop out the seeds, and cut into 2-inch (5-cm) pieces. Boil the cucumbers for 3 minutes, drain, and cool under cold running water.

Return the curry base to a simmer over medium heat. Cut the fish into 2-inch (5-cm) cubes and add to the base along with the clams (discarding any that do not close to the touch) and cucumbers. Simmer until the fish is opaque throughout, about 8 minutes. Add the shrimp, scallops, and squid during the last 3 minutes of cooking; the shrimp should be bright pink and the scallops and squid opaque throughout when they are done.

Spoon the stew into a warmed serving bowl, discarding any clams that failed to open. Garnish with the mint and cilantro and serve at once.

Serves 4

2 teaspoons ground coriander

1 teaspoon ground cumin

3 tablespoons peanut oil

1 yellow onion, finely minced

1 tablespoon *each* peeled and grated fresh ginger and finely minced garlic

2 teaspoons *each* grated lime zest and minced lemongrass

1–2 teaspoons seeded and minced jalapeño chile

2 cups (16 fl oz/500 ml) unsweetened coconut milk

1½ cups (12 fl oz/375 ml) fish broth or clam juice

¼ cup (⅓ oz/10 g) fresh cilantro (fresh coriander), puréed with 1 tablespoon water

1 tablespoon fresh lime juice

1 tablespoon firmly packed golden brown sugar

Salt and freshly ground pepper

2 small squid

2 small cucumbers, peeled

1 lb (500 g) firm white fish fillets

24 clams, well scrubbed

8 *each* medium shrimp (prawns), peeled and deveined, and sea scallops

¼ cup (⅓ oz/10 g) *each* chopped fresh mint and cilantro

Caramelized Shrimp with Sour Bean Sprouts

In Vietnam, caramel sauce is primarily used to enrich savory dishes rather than desserts. Sour bean sprouts, a perfect union of sweet, salty, and tart flavors, are the traditional accompaniment and ideal match for caramelized dishes.

FOR THE BEAN SPROUTS:

1/2 cup (4 fl oz/125 ml) white vinegar

2 tablespoons granulated sugar

1 tablespoon salt

1 lb (500 g) mung bean sprouts

1 carrot, peeled and julienned

1/3 cup (2 1/2 oz/75 g) firmly packed golden brown sugar

1 teaspoon lemon juice

1 lb (500g) large shrimp (prawns)

2 tablespoons fish sauce

2 teaspoons granulated sugar

1 teaspoon peeled and minced fresh ginger

1/4 teaspoon freshly ground pepper

1 1/2 tablespoons peanut oil

2 cloves garlic, minced

3 large shallots, sliced

2 green (spring) onions, cut into 2-inch (5-cm) pieces

1 tablespoon lime juice

To make the bean sprouts, in a saucepan over high heat, combine 4 cups (32 fl oz/1 l) water, the vinegar, granulated sugar, and salt and bring to a boil. Let cool. Place the bean sprouts and carrot in a large glass bowl, pour in the vinegar mixture, cover, and let stand at room temperature for 1 hour. Drain and set aside.

In a small, heavy saucepan over high heat, combine the brown sugar and 1/4 cup (2 fl oz/60 ml) water and bring to a boil. Cook, maintaining a steady boil, until the mixture forms small, sluggish, rich brown bubbles, 5–8 minutes. Immediately remove from the heat and stir in another 1/4 cup (2 fl oz/60 ml) water. Bring to a gentle boil over medium-high heat and cook until the caramel is completely dissolved, about 5 minutes longer. Add the lemon juice and set aside. You should have about 1/3 cup (3 fl oz/80 ml) caramel sauce. (Extra sauce will keep indefinitely in the refrigerator.)

Peel and devein the shrimp. In a bowl, toss the shrimp with the fish sauce, sugar, ginger, and pepper. In a wok or small saucepan over medium heat, warm the oil. Add the garlic and shallots and sauté until golden, about 1 minute. Remove the shrimp from the marinade, reserving the marinade. Raise the heat to medium-high, add the shrimp, and cook until bright pink, about 2 minutes. Add the green onions, the reserved marinade, and 2 tablespoons of the caramel sauce and stir to coat evenly. Stir in the lime juice.

To serve, divide the shrimp mixture among serving bowls and pass the bean sprouts and carrots at the table.

Serves 4

Beef Braised in Star Anise Sauce

This "red-braised" stew is a popular Chinese home-style dish. "Red" refers to the reddish brown color, acquired from the use of dark soy sauce. Serve with steamed white or jasmine rice and a green vegetable.

Cut the beef into irregular 1½-inch (4-cm) chunks. In a large bowl, combine the beef chunks with the 1 tablespoon soy sauce, 1 tablespoon of the cornstarch, and the 1 teaspoon sugar. Toss to coat the beef evenly.

In a Dutch oven over medium-high heat, warm the oil. Add the green onions, garlic, ginger, and salt and sauté until fragrant, about 30 seconds. Add the beef in small batches and sauté until browned, about 10 minutes each. Add the wine, the ¼ cup (2 fl oz/60 ml) soy sauce, the 2 tablespoons sugar, the star anise, and enough water to cover the meat. Bring to a boil, cover, reduce the heat to low, and simmer for about 1 hour.

Cut the carrots and daikon into irregular 1-inch (2.5-cm) chunks. Add the carrots and daikon to the pot and simmer until the beef and vegetables are tender, about 30 minutes longer. Remove the garlic cloves and ginger pieces and discard. Mix the remaining 1½ tablespoons cornstarch with 3 tablespoons water. Add the cornstarch mixture to the pot and cook, stirring occasionally, until the sauce thickens, about 30 seconds. Stir in the sesame oil.

To serve, divide the beef and vegetables among the serving bowls and serve at once.

Serves 6

2½ lb (1.25 kg) boneless beef chuck

1 tablespoon dark soy sauce, plus ¼ cup (2 fl oz/60 ml)

2½ tablespoon cornstarch (cornflour)

1 teaspoon granulated sugar, plus 2 tablespoons

2 tablespoons corn oil

4 green (spring) onions, including the tender green tops, cut into 2-inch (5-cm) pieces

4 cloves garlic, crushed

2 inches (5 cm) fresh ginger, peeled and crushed

1 teaspoon salt

¼ cup (2 fl oz/60 ml) Chinese rice wine or dry sherry

6 whole star anise pods

2 carrots, peeled

1½ lb (750 g) daikon or turnips, peeled

1 teaspoon Asian sesame oil

Baked Swordfish with Tomato-Caper Sauce

Vary this dish by adding a few chopped olives or anchovies to the sauce, or by replacing the swordfish with tuna or halibut. On another occasion, try the sauce on spaghetti. Doubling the sauce will make enough for ¼ pound (125 g) pasta.

4 swordfish steaks, 6 oz (185 g) and ½ inch (12 mm) thick each

Salt and freshly ground pepper

3 tablespoons olive oil, plus 2 teaspoons

3 small cloves garlic, minced

Large pinch of red pepper flakes

2 cups (12 oz/370 g) grated plum (Roma) tomatoes

2 teaspoons chopped fresh oregano

1 tablespoon rinsed and chopped capers

¼ cup (2 fl oz/60 ml) dry white wine

Preheat the oven to 400°F (200°C).

Season the swordfish generously with salt and pepper. Put the 3 tablespoons olive oil in a small baking dish. Add the swordfish and turn to coat with the oil. Set aside.

In a small frying pan over medium heat, warm the 2 teaspoons olive oil. Add the garlic and sauté for 1 minute to release its fragrance. Add the red pepper flakes, tomatoes, and oregano and simmer until the mixture is thick and saucelike, about 5 minutes. Stir in the capers. Season to taste with salt. Remove from the heat.

Drizzle the white wine around the fish, then bake until the fish is opaque throughout when pierced with a knife, 10–12 minutes.

Using a spatula, transfer the fish to warmed individual plates. Reheat the sauce gently, adding a few drops of water, if needed, to thin it a bit, then spoon the sauce over the fish. Serve at once.

Serves 4

Indian Chicken Curry

The classic flavors of India come to the table in this simple chicken curry, which is served with an array of condiments. For a lighter curry, substitute an additional 1½ cups (12 fl oz/375 ml) stock for the coconut milk. Serve with steamed rice.

6–8 tablespoons (2¼–2½ oz/ 67–75 g) all-purpose (plain) flour

4 skinless chicken breast halves, about ½ lb (250 g) each

4 skinless chicken thighs, about 6 oz (185 g) each

4 skinless chicken drumsticks, about 4 oz (125 g) each

1 lb (500 g) chicken wings

2 tablespoons canola or safflower oil

2 yellow onions, chopped

2 cloves garlic, finely chopped

2–4 tablespoons curry powder

1½ cups (12 fl oz/375 ml) Chicken Stock (page 288) or broth

1½ cups (12 fl oz/375 ml) coconut milk

Salt and freshly ground pepper

Condiments: Mango chutney, diced tomato, chopped green (spring) onions, banana slices, chopped peanuts, unsweetened dried shredded coconut

Spread the flour on a plate, then lightly coat both sides of each chicken piece with the flour, shaking off the excess.

In a Dutch oven or other large pot over high heat, warm the oil. Add the chicken pieces in batches and sauté, turning once, until browned, about 2 minutes on each side. Transfer to a plate and set aside.

Reduce the heat to medium, add the onions to the pot, and sauté until softened, about 2 minutes. Stir in the garlic and curry powder to taste and sauté, stirring, for 1 minute longer. Raise the heat to high, stir in the stock, and deglaze the pot, stirring to scrape up any browned bits from the bottom.

Return the chicken to the pot and bring to a boil. Add the coconut milk, reduce the heat to low, cover, and simmer until the chicken is opaque throughout, about 20 minutes. Season to taste with salt and pepper.

Transfer the chicken and sauce to a warmed serving bowl. Arrange the condiments in small bowls for diners to add as desired.

Serves 6–8

Chicken Cacciatore

Chicken cacciatore, or "hunter's style" chicken, is an old-fashioned Italian favorite. Fresh herbs, mushrooms, and tomatoes make this contemporary version particularly aromatic and hearty. Serve with buttered pasta.

Dust the chicken pieces with the paprika. In a heavy frying pan or Dutch oven over high heat, warm the olive oil. Add the chicken in batches and cook, turning once, until browned, about 2 minutes on each side. Transfer to a plate and set aside. Season to taste with salt and pepper to taste.

Pour off all but 2 tablespoons of the fat from the pan and place over medium heat. Add the onion and sauté until softened, about 2 minutes. Stir in the garlic and mushrooms and sauté until the mushrooms are softened, 1–2 minutes longer. Sprinkle the flour over the mushrooms and stir to incorporate and slightly cook the flour. Stir in the marjoram, basil, and thyme.

Raise the heat to high, pour in the stock and wine, and deglaze the pan, stirring to scrape up any browned bits from the pan bottom. Add the tomatoes, stir well, and bring to a boil. Return the chicken to the pan and stir to combine with the sauce. Cover and reduce the heat to medium-low. Cook, stirring occasionally, until the chicken is opaque throughout, about 25 minutes.

Using tongs, transfer the chicken pieces to a warmed platter. Spoon the sauce over the top and serve at once.

Serves 4

2 skinless chicken breast halves, 8 oz (250 g) each

2 skinless chicken thighs, about 6 oz (185 g) each

2 skinless chicken drumsticks, about 4 oz (125 g) each

2 chicken wings

1 tablespoon paprika

2 tablespoons olive oil

Salt and freshly ground pepper

1 yellow onion, chopped

3 cloves garlic, minced

1/2 lb (250 g) fresh cremini mushrooms, cleaned and sliced

2 tablespoons all-purpose (plain) flour

1 tablespoon *each* chopped fresh marjoram, basil, and thyme

1 cup (8 fl oz/250 ml) Chicken Stock (page 288) or broth

1 cup (8 fl oz/250 ml) dry red wine

5 tomatoes, peeled, seeded, and chopped

Spinach, Corn, and Potato Enchiladas

Many enchilada recipes call for frying the tortillas, but in this healthier version they are dipped into the sauce without frying first. Do not leave the tortillas in the sauce for too long, as they will fall apart.

2 large russet potatoes

1/2 cup (3 oz/90 g) corn kernels

1 large red bell pepper (capsicum), seeded and diced

1 yellow onion, coarsely chopped

10 oz (315 g) spinach leaves, thinly sliced

1 can (28 fl oz/875 ml) enchilada sauce

Salt and freshly ground pepper

12 corn tortillas

1/4 lb (125 g) Cheddar cheese, shredded

Preheat the oven to 375°F (190°C).

Place the potatoes on a baking sheet and bake until tender when pierced with the tip of a sharp knife, 40–45 minutes. Let cool completely, then dice and set aside.

Reduce the oven temperature to 350°F (180°C).

In a saucepan, combine the diced potatoes, corn, bell pepper, onion, and spinach. Add 1 cup (8 fl oz/250 ml) of the enchilada sauce and mix well. Place over medium heat, cover tightly, and cook until the spinach is wilted, 5–6 minutes. Remove from the heat, season to taste with salt and pepper, and set aside.

Spread about 1/2 cup (4 fl oz/125 ml) of the remaining enchilada sauce into a 9-by-13-inch (23-by-33-cm) baking dish. It should just cover the bottom.

In a wide frying pan over medium heat, warm the remaining enchilada sauce. One at a time, dip each tortilla into the warm sauce, allowing it to warm just enough to become pliable. Then, place it in the prepared baking dish, and spoon about one-twelfth of the potato-corn mixture along its center. Roll up the tortilla and arrange it in the dish, seam side down. Repeat with remaining tortillas and filling. The dish should be tightly packed.

Pour any sauce remaining in the pan over the enchiladas. Sprinkle with the Cheddar cheese. Bake, uncovered, until the cheese is melted and the surface is browned, 15–20 minutes. Let cool for 15 minutes, then serve at once.

Serves 6

Eggplant Parmesan

Look for Asian eggplants when making this recipe, but the more familiar globe eggplant would certainly work. Eggplant lends itself to quick preparation, and is often served in place of meat.

Preheat the broiler (griller).

Trim the ends off the eggplants, then cut lengthwise into slices ¹/₄ inch (6 mm) thick. Lightly brush both sides of the eggplant slices with 3 tablespoons olive oil and arrange on a baking sheet. Season to taste with salt and pepper to taste. Place the eggplant under the broiler and broil (grill) until lightly browned on the first side, 4–5 minutes. Turn and broil until lightly browned on the second side, about 4 minutes longer. Transfer the slices to paper towels to drain.

Reduce the heat to 375°F (190°C).

In a small frying pan over medium heat, warm the 3 teaspoons olive oil. Add the garlic and sauté for 1 minute to release its fragrance. Add the tomatoes and basil and season to taste with salt and pepper. Simmer briskly, stirring often, until the mixture forms a sauce, about 5 minutes. Remove from the heat.

Choose a nonaluminum baking dish just large enough to hold the eggplant in 2 layers. Arrange half of the eggplant in the baking dish, then spread with half of the tomato sauce. Top with half of the mozzarella. Repeat the layers, then top with the Parmesan cheese.

Bake until it is bubbling hot and the cheese is nicely browned, about 20 minutes. Let cool for 10 minutes before serving.

Serves 4

6 Asian eggplants (slender aubergines), each about 2–4 oz (185–250 g)

3 tablespoons olive oil, plus 3 teaspoons

Salt and freshly ground pepper

3 cloves garlic, minced

1 cup (6 oz/185 g) chopped plum (Roma) tomatoes

8 fresh basil leaves, torn into small pieces

1 cup (2¹/₂ oz/75 g) shredded whole-milk mozzarella cheese

¹/₄ cup grated Parmesan cheese

Baked Spanish Rice with Chicken, Shrimp, and Mussels

1 bay leaf

1/2 cup (1 oz/30 g) chopped celery leaves

1/4 yellow onion, plus 1 yellow onion, chopped

Salt

1 whole chicken breast, about 1 lb (500 g), skinned

1 cup (5 oz/155 g) shelled peas

2 cups (14 oz/440 g) long-grain white rice

2 tablespoons pure olive oil

1 green bell pepper (capsicum), seeded and chopped

3 cloves garlic, minced

3 1/2 cups (28 fl oz/875 ml) water

1 cup (8 fl oz/250 ml) tomato sauce

1 tablespoon chopped fresh oregano

3 saffron threads

Freshly ground pepper

1–2 lb (500 g–1 kg) mussels, well scrubbed and debearded

1/2 cup (4 fl oz/125 ml) dry white wine or water

1/2 lb (250 g) medium-sized shrimp (prawns), peeled and deveined

1/2 cup (3/4 oz/20 g) chopped fresh flat-leaf (Italian) parsley

Fill a saucepan two-thirds full with water. Add the bay leaf, celery leaves, 1/4 onion, and 1 teaspoon salt. Bring to a boil, add the chicken, and reduce the heat to medium. Simmer, uncovered, until the chicken is opaque throughout, about 15 minutes. Transfer the chicken to a plate, let cool, remove the meat from the bones, and cut in to cubes. Meanwhile, bring another saucepan three-fourths full of water to a boil. Add the peas and boil until barely tender, 2–3 minutes. Rinse with cold running water to stop the cooking, drain, and set aside.

Preheat the oven to 350°F (180°C). Butter a shallow 2-qt (2-l) baking dish. Rinse the rice, changing the water until it runs clear. In a frying pan over medium-high heat, warm the oil. Add the chopped onion and bell pepper and sauté until softened, about 3 minutes. Stir in the garlic and sauté until fragrant, about 20 seconds longer. Stir in the rice and sauté for about 2 minutes. Add 3 1/2 cups (28 fl oz/875 ml) water, the tomato sauce, oregano, and saffron. Season to taste with salt and pepper and stir well. Bring to a boil and pour into the prepared baking dish.

Cover and bake for 20 minutes. Remove from the oven, uncover, and stir in the cooked chicken and peas. Re-cover, return the dish to the oven, and continue baking until the rice is tender and all the liquid is absorbed, 10–15 minutes longer.

Meanwhile, prepare the seafood: In a wide saucepan over medium-high heat, combine the mussels and wine, discarding any mussels that do not close to the touch. Cover and bring to a boil. Cook until the mussels open, 3–5 minutes. Remove from the heat and discard any mussels that failed to open; keep warm. In another saucepan, bring 2 cups (16 fl oz/500 ml) water to a boil over high heat. Add the shrimp and cook until they turn pink, about 3 minutes. Drain and keep warm.

Remove the rice from the oven and uncover. Arrange the mussels and shrimp on top, sprinkle with the parsley, and serve at once.

Serves 4–6

Chicken and Asparagus with Spicy Black Bean Sauce

This stir-fry is especially delicious poured over a plate of steamed rice. Chinese preserved black beans are salted fermented black soybeans. When stir-fried, they exude a pungent and rich savory flavor. Use asparagus that is not too thin and not too fat.

Snap off the tough ends of the asparagus where they break naturally and discard; cut the spears on the diagonal into 1½-inch (4-cm) pieces. Thinly slice the onion. Cut the red bell pepper into ½-inch (12-mm) cubes. Cut the chicken into ½-inch (12-mm) dice. Place all the ingredients in small bowls near the stove.

In a wok or frying pan over medium-high heat, warm the oil. Add the garlic, black beans, ginger, and salt and toss and stir until fragrant, about 1 minute. Raise the heat to high, add the asparagus, onion, and bell pepper, and toss and stir until coated with oil and seared, about 1 minute.

Add the chicken and toss and stir until opaque throughout and firm, about 2 minutes. Add the stock, soy sauce, sugar, and chile, bring to a boil, cover, and cook until the asparagus is tender but still crunchy, about 1 minute longer. Add the cornstarch mixture and the oyster sauce, if using, and cook, stirring continuously, until the sauce thickens, about 30 seconds. Stir in the sesame oil.

To serve, divide the stir-fry among warmed individual plates and serve at once.

Serves 4

3/4 lb (375 g) skinless, boneless, chicken thighs

3/4 lb (375 g) asparagus spears

1/2 yellow onion, thinly sliced

1/2 red bell pepper (capsicum)

1½ tablespoons peanut oil

2 cloves garlic, chopped

2 tablespoons Chinese preserved black beans, rinsed with cold water and drained

1 teaspoon peeled and chopped fresh ginger

1/2 teaspoon salt

3/4 cup (6 fl oz/180 ml) Chicken Stock (page 288) or broth

1 tablespoon soy sauce

1/2 teaspoon sugar

1 red jalapeño chile, seeded and chopped

1½ tablespoons cornstarch (cornflour) mixed with 2 tablespoons water

1 teaspoon oyster sauce (optional)

1 teaspoon Asian sesame oil

Beef with Thai Basil and Jasmine Rice

Thai, or holy, basil has distinctive deep purple stems, dark green leaves, and lavender blossoms. Its anise-like flavor is more perfumed and less tart than that of Italian basil. Here it adds its fragrance and flavor to a quick, Thai-style stir-fry.

2 tablespoons Chinese preserved black beans, rinsed with cold water and drained

4 cloves garlic, minced

1 piece fresh ginger, 1½ inches (4 cm), peeled and minced

2 tablespoons dry sherry, plus 1 teaspoon

3 teaspoons soy sauce

2 teaspoons cornstarch (cornflour)

½ teaspoon sugar

Salt

1 lb (500 g) beef top sirloin, about 1 inch (2.5 cm) thick, sliced paper-thin across the grain

3 tablespoons peanut oil

1 cup (7 oz/220 g) jasmine rice

¼ cup (⅓ oz/10 g) chopped fresh Thai basil

In a small bowl, stir together the black beans, garlic, ginger, the 2 tablespoons sherry, and 1 teaspoon of the soy sauce. Set aside.

In a bowl large enough to hold the beef, combine the remaining 2 teaspoons soy sauce, the 1 teaspoon sherry, the cornstarch, sugar, and ¼ teaspoon salt. Stir until well mixed, then add the beef and stir to coat evenly. Pour 1 tablespoon of the peanut oil over the beef, mix well, and marinate at room temperature for 30 minutes.

While the beef is marinating, cook the rice: In a heavy saucepan over medium-high heat, bring 2 cups (16 fl oz/500 ml) water to a boil. Add 1 teaspoon salt and the rice. When the water returns to a boil, reduce the heat to low, cover, and cook until the rice is tender and the water has been fully absorbed, about 20 minutes.

About 5 minutes before the rice is ready, in a wok or large, deep frying pan over high heat, heat the remaining 2 tablespoons oil. When the oil is very hot, add the beef and its marinade and toss and stir until the meat has changed color but is still pink, 2–3 minutes. Pour in the black bean mixture and continue to toss and stir just until the meat is barely cooked through, 1–2 minutes longer. Stir in half of the basil.

To serve, mound the rice in a warmed serving bowl or divide evenly among warmed individual bowls or plates and top with the beef. Garnish with the remaining basil.

Serves 4

Texas-Style Chili

On a weekend when friends have gathered to watch a big game, offer bowls of this pleasantly spicy chili along with plenty of ice-cold beer and homemade corn bread. Set out bowls of the garnishes for a self-service chili bar.

Cut the beef into 3/4-inch (2-cm) cubes and pat dry. In large, heavy deep-sided pot, pour in enough vegetable oil to form a film on the bottom; place over medium heat. When hot, add the meat, in batches, in a single layer. Cook, turning often, until the beef is browned on all sides, 3–5 minutes. Transfer to a plate and repeat until all the meat is browned, adding more oil as needed.

Add more oil to the pot to coat the bottom and place over medium heat. Add the carrots, onions, and garlic and cook, stirring, until the vegetables are slightly softened, about 2 minutes. Return the browned meat to the pot and sprinkle the meat and vegetables with the flour. Cook, stirring vigorously, for 1 minute. Add the chili powder, cumin, oregano, salt, red pepper flakes, tomatoes, 5 cups (40 fl oz/ 1.25 l) of the stock, and the chipotle chiles. Bring to a simmer, then reduce the heat to low, cover, and cook for about 30 minutes. Uncover and continue to cook until the meat is fork tender, 1 1/2–2 hours longer. If the chili becomes too thick, thin with as much of the remaining 1 cup (8 fl oz/250 ml) stock as needed. Taste and adjust the seasonings. Remove and discard the chipotle chiles.

Rinse and drain the beans, then pat dry. In a large, heavy frying pan over medium high heat, warm 2 teaspoons vegetable oil. Add the beans and cook, stirring, until hot, 2–3 minutes. Divide the beans among shallow soup bowls and ladle the chili over them. Let your guests garnish bowls of chili as they like with the cheese, sour cream, and cilantro.

Serves 6

3 lb (1.5 kg) lean beef stew meat, trimmed of excess fat

Vegetable oil

2 carrots, peeled and finely diced

2 yellow onions, chopped

4 teaspoons chopped garlic

3 tablespoons all-purpose (plain) flour

1/4 cup (2 oz/60 g) chili powder

3 1/2 teaspoons ground cumin

2 1/4 teaspoons dried oregano

1 1/2 teaspoons salt

1/4 teaspoon red pepper flakes

2 cans (28 oz/875 g each) plum (Roma) tomatoes, drained and chopped

5–6 cups (40–48 fl oz/1.25–1.5 l) Beef Stock (page 288) or broth

2 chipotle chiles

2 cans (15 oz/470 g each) black beans

Garnishes: Shredded Monterey jack cheese, sour cream, and chopped fresh cilantro (fresh coriander)

Dry Beef Curry

The sauce for this stew is dry, meaning that it coats the meat at the end of cooking. The recipe calls for ten to fifteen dried red chiles. Serve with steamed rice to temper the heat. Accompany with a cooling pineapple–cilantro–red chile salsa.

10–15 dried red chiles, seeded

5 blanched almonds

6 shallots, chopped

4 cloves garlic, chopped

3 slices fresh galangal, chopped

4 stalks lemongrass, center white part only, chopped

4 slices peeled fresh ginger, chopped

1 teaspoon anchovy paste

1¹/₂ teaspoons *each* ground coriander and ground cumin

¹/₄ teaspoon *each* turmeric, ground fennel and ground cloves

¹/₄ cup (1 oz/30 g) unsweetened shredded dried coconut

2¹/₄ lb (1.25 kg) beef chuck

2 tablespoons vegetable oil

1 cinnamon stick

1 can (13¹/₂ fl oz/425 ml) unsweetened coconut milk

1 tablespoon *each* soy sauce and sugar

1 teaspoon salt

Place the chiles in a small bowl, add warm water to cover, and let stand until soft, 10 minutes. Meanwhile, place the almonds in a small bowl, add warm water to cover, and let stand until moist, about 5 minutes. Drain the chiles and almonds.

In a blender, combine the chiles, almonds, shallots, garlic, galangal, three-fourths of the lemongrass, the ginger, anchovy paste, coriander, cumin, turmeric, fennel, and cloves. Add 2 tablespoons water or just enough to facilitate blending. Process until a smooth paste forms. Set aside. In a small, dry frying pan over medium heat, toast the coconut until golden brown, 3–5 minutes. Transfer to a plate and let cool.

Cut the beef chuck into 1-inch (2.5-cm) cubes and set aside. In a Dutch oven over medium-high heat, warm the oil. Add the spice paste and cook, stirring constantly, until the paste is aromatic and beads of oil separate from the paste, 3–5 minutes. Add the cinnamon stick, toasted coconut, and remaining chopped lemongrass, and cook, stirring occasionally, for 1 minute. Add the beef and toss and stir to coat the cubes evenly, about 5 minutes. Add the coconut milk, soy sauce, sugar, and salt and bring to a boil, stirring constantly. Reduce the heat to low and simmer, uncovered, stirring occasionally, until the meat is tender, 1–1¹/₂ hours. If the sauce begins to dry out before the meat is done, add a little hot water to thin it.

Raise the heat to medium-high and cook until the sauce is thick, 5–10 minutes. Fry the meat in the sauce until lightly browned, about 5 minutes. The sauce should coat the meat. Divide among warmed individual bowls and serve hot.

Serves 6

Hoisin Chicken with Noodles

Yakisoba are fresh Japanese wheat noodles that are a bit thicker than vermicelli. Look for them in Asian markets and well-stocked groceries. Garnish with chopped green (spring) onion tops for a splash of color.

In a saucepan, bring 3 cups (24 fl oz/750 ml) water to a boil. Place the noodles in a large heatproof bowl and pour the boiling water over them. Let the noodles stand for 5 minutes, then drain and pat dry. Toss the noodles with 1 teaspoon of the five-spice powder.

In a 14-inch (35-cm) nonstick frying pan over medium-high heat, warm 1 tablespoon of the olive oil. Add the noodles, forming them into a cake that covers the bottom of the pan. Cook until browned on the first side, about 6 minutes. Turn over the noodle cake and cook until browned and crisp on the second side, about 6 minutes longer. Slide the noodle cake out of the pan onto a work surface. Cut into 4 equal wedges and keep warm.

Return the pan to the heat and warm the remaining 1 tablespoon olive oil. Add the leeks, eggplants, mushrooms, carrots, and the remaining 1 teaspoon five-spice powder. Toss and stir until the vegetables are just beginning to soften, about 10 minutes.

Add the chicken, ginger, and garlic. Cover the pan and cook until the chicken is opaque throughout, about 3 minutes. Add the hoisin sauce and 1/2 cup (4 fl oz/ 125 ml) cold water and toss and stir until all the ingredients are well coated, about 1 minute longer.

Divide the chicken mixture evenly among warmed plates and top with the noodle wedges. Serve at once.

Serves 4

3/4 lb (375 g) yakisoba noodles

2 teaspoons Chinese five-spice powder

2 tablespoons olive oil

2 1/2 cups (10 oz/315 g) julienned leeks

3 Asian eggplants (slender aubergines), thinly sliced

6 oz (185 g) fresh shiitake mushrooms, brushed clean, stemmed and sliced

2 cups (10 oz/310 g) shredded carrots

1 lb (500 g) chicken tenders, thinly sliced crosswise

3 tablespoons peeled and minced fresh ginger

2 large cloves garlic, minced

6 tablespoons (3 fl oz/90 ml) hoisin sauce

Chicken Fajitas with Guacamole

Leftover chicken can be substituted here; stir it in after all the other ingredients are cooked and then heat through before serving. Seed the chile for a more mild version of this dish. Use homemade tomato salsa or a good-quality purchased version.

Preheat the oven to 200°F (95°C).

Wrap the tortillas in aluminum foil and place in the warm, about 10 minutes.

Meanwhile, in a frying pan over medium-high heat, warm the oil. Add the chicken and sauté until opaque throughout and firm, about 4 minutes. Using a slotted spoon, transfer the chicken to a plate and set aside.

Add the onion and red and green bell peppers to the oil remaining in the pan and sauté over medium-high heat until softened, about 4 minutes. Stir in the chile, oregano, cumin, and garlic and sauté until the garlic is softened, about 20 seconds. Stir in the 2 tablespoons salsa and 1/2 cup (4 fl oz/125 ml) water and bring to a boil. Add the tomatoes and season to taste with salt and pepper. Cook, uncovered, until the liquid evaporates, about 5 minutes. Return the chicken to the pan, mix well, and heat to serving temperature. Transfer to a warmed serving platter.

To serve, remove the tortillas from the oven and place the 3/4 cup (6 fl oz/180 ml) salsa in a small bowl. Set the chicken, tortillas, salsa, and guacamole on the table and let diners assemble their own fajitas.

Serves 4

8–12 small (6 inches/15 cm) corn or flour tortillas

2 tablespoons canola oil

1 lb (500 g) skinless, boneless chicken breast halves, cut into thin strips

1 yellow onion, halved and sliced

1/2 red bell pepper (capsicum), seeded and thinly sliced

1/2 green bell pepper (capsicum), seeded and thinly sliced

1 jalapeño chile, seeded, if desired, and finely chopped

2 teaspoons chopped fresh oregano

1/2 teaspoon ground cumin

2 cloves garlic, minced

2 tablespoons tomato salsa, plus 3/4 cup (6 fl oz/180 ml)

2 plum (Roma) tomatoes, seeded and chopped

Salt and freshly ground pepper

3/4 cup (6 oz/185g) prepared guacamole

Chicken with Lemon, Garlic, and Parsley

Offer this refreshing dish on a hot summer's night. A garnish of lemon zest, parsley, and garlic recalls the gremolata that traditionally tops Milan's famed osso buco. For an extra spark of aroma, taste, and color, substitute orange zest for half of the lemon zest.

2 tablespoons all-purpose (plain) flour

4 skinless, boneless chicken breast halves, about 1/2 lb (250 g) each

3–5 cloves garlic

3/4 cup (1/2 oz/15 g) chopped fresh flat-leaf (Italian) parsley

1 tablespoon finely chopped lemon zest

2 tablespoons olive oil

Salt and freshly ground pepper

3/4 cup (6 fl oz/180 ml) Chicken Stock (page 288) or broth

1/2 cup (4 fl oz/125 ml) fresh lemon juice

1/2 cup (4 fl oz/125 ml) dry white wine

Spread the flour on a plate, then lightly coat both sides of each chicken breast half with the flour, shaking off the excess. Finely chop 2 or 3 garlic cloves, then mince 1 or 2 additional cloves. Set aside the chopped garlic. In a small bowl, stir together the minced garlic to taste, the parsley, and lemon zest.

In a frying pan over high heat, warm the olive oil. Add the chicken breasts and sauté, turning once, until lightly browned, about 2 minutes on each side. Transfer to a platter, season to taste with salt and pepper to taste, and set aside.

Pour off all but 2 tablespoons of the fat from the pan. Add the finely chopped garlic to taste to the pan and sauté over high heat until softened, about 20 seconds. Add the stock, lemon juice, and wine and deglaze the pan, stirring to scrape up any browned bits from the pan bottom. Bring to a boil and cook until slightly reduced, about 3 minutes.

Return the chicken to the pan and reduce the heat to medium. Cook until the chicken is opaque throughout and the juices run clear when a breast half is pierced with a knife, about 10 minutes. Using tongs, transfer the chicken to a warmed serving platter.

Raise the heat to high and boil the pan sauce until reduced to about 1/4 cup (2 fl oz/60 ml), about 5 minutes. Pour the sauce evenly over the chicken and sprinkle the parsley-garlic mixture evenly over the top. Serve at once.

Serves 4

Sides

Summer Squash with Mint Pesto

For a dish with more dramatic contrasts of color, use only the squash flesh that includes some of the colored skin. In this case, you will need about 8 green and 8 yellow squashes. Use the remaining squash as a stuffing for vegetables.

1 cup (1½ oz/45 g) firmly packed fresh mint leaves

⅓ cup (3 fl oz/80 ml) Vegetable Stock (page 289) or broth

3 tablespoons grated Asiago cheese, plus more for garnish, (optional)

2 large cloves garlic, coarsely chopped

2 teaspoons olive oil, plus tablespoon plus

3 yellow crookneck squashes, about ¾ lb (375 g) total weight

3 zucchini (courgettes), about ¾ lb (375 g) total weight

1 shallot, finely diced

1 tablespoon chopped fresh thyme

Salt and freshly ground pepper

In a blender or food processor, combine the mint, stock, 2 tablespoons of the Asiago cheese, the garlic, and 2 teaspoons of the olive oil. Process until smooth. Set aside.

Using a mandoline or a vegetable peeler, cut the yellow squashes and zucchini into long, narrow ribbons.

In a large, nonstick frying pan over medium heat, warm the 1 tablespoon olive oil. Add the shallot and sauté until softened, about 3 minutes. Add the yellow squashes and zucchini and the thyme and season generously with salt and pepper. Sauté until the squashes are just tender, about 8 minutes.

Stir in the pesto and heat for 1 minute. Remove from the heat and stir in the remaining 1 tablespoon Asiago cheese.

Transfer to a warmed serving dish and toss with extra cheese, if you like. Serve hot.

Serves 4–6

Old-Fashioned Potato Salad

This salad can be prepared up to 8 hours in advance, covered, and refrigerated. Bring to room temperature before serving. You can quickly turn this side dish into a main course by adding diced ham or roast chicken.

In a saucepan, combine the potatoes with water to cover. Bring to a boil over high heat and boil until just barely tender, about 20 minutes. Drain, rinse under cold running water, and drain again. Let cool slightly.

Peel the potatoes and cut them in half lengthwise. Cut each half into slices about $1/4$ inch (6 mm) thick. In a large bowl, combine the potatoes, dill pickles, eggs, and celery.

In a small bowl, mash together the garlic and $1/2$ teaspoon salt with the back of a spoon to form a paste. Stir in the lemon juice, mustard, paprika, and cayenne pepper. Whisk in the mayonnaise and olive oil to make a dressing. Pour the dressing over the potato mixture and toss gently to mix. Season to taste with salt and pepper. Cover and refrigerate until needed. Remove from the refrigerator about 30 minutes before serving.

Serve the potato salad slightly chilled or at room temperature. Sprinkle with the parsley just before serving.

Serves 6

2 lb (1 kg) boiling potatoes (about 4 potatoes)

$1/2$ cup (3 oz/90 g) chopped dill pickles

4 hard-boiled eggs, peeled and coarsely chopped

1 celery rib, finely chopped

1 large clove garlic, minced

Salt

2 tablespoons fresh lemon juice

2 teaspoons Dijon mustard

1 teaspoon Hungarian sweet paprika

$1/8$ teaspoon cayenne pepper

$2/3$ cup (5 fl oz/160 ml) mayonnaise

$1/4$ cup (2 fl oz/60 ml) olive oil

Freshly ground black pepper

1 tablespoon chopped fresh flat-leaf (Italian) parsley

Stir-fried Pea Shoots with Garlic

Pea shoots, the curly tendrils and top pair of leaves of young green pea plants, have a delicate, sweet flavor. Look for pea shoots in Asian markets; if they are unavailable, substitute spinach or watercress.

1 lb (500 g) pea shoots

2 tablespoons peanut oil

3 cloves garlic, chopped

1 slice fresh ginger, peeled and crushed

$1/2$ teaspoon salt

2 tablespoons Chicken Stock (page 288) or broth

Pinch of sugar

Asian sesame oil for drizzling

Rinse the pea shoots in cold running water. Drain and dry in a salad spinner or thoroughly pat dry with paper towels.

Warm a wok or frying pan over medium heat. Add the oil, garlic, ginger, and salt and toss and stir until fragrant, about 30 seconds. Raise the heat to high, add 2 or 3 handfuls of the pea shoots, and toss and stir until wilted, again about 30 seconds. Push the shoots up the sides of the wok and add another 2 or 3 handfuls. Toss and stir until wilted, about 30 seconds. Push the shoots up the sides of the wok and repeat until all the pea shoots have been added to the wok and cooked. If water accumulates in the bottom of the wok, push the shoots up the sides to allow the liquid to reduce. Add the stock and sugar and toss and stir until the liquid is reduced to a few tablespoons, 1–2 minutes. Drizzle to taste with sesame oil.

Transfer the pea shoots to a bowl and serve at once.

Serves 4

Swiss Chard with Pine Nuts

Serve this invitingly simple wilted salad before any pasta except one that includes leafy greens. This recipe can also be made with spinach leaves. For a sweet accent, try tossing in some golden raisins.

Trim the chard ribs from the leaves and wash them separately. Drain the leaves in a colander. Cut the ribs into $^{1}/_{4}$-inch (6-mm) pieces.

Bring a pot three-fourths full of salted water to a boil. Add the chard ribs and cook until tender, 3–5 minutes. Drain.

Meanwhile, put the chard leaves in a large frying pan with just the rinsing water clinging to them. Place over medium heat, cover, and cook, stirring once or twice, until they wilt, about 5 minutes. Uncover and continue to cook to evaporate any excess moisture. Stir in the chard ribs, then remove from the heat.

In a small, dry frying pan over medium-low heat, warm together the olive oil and pine nuts. Toast the nuts in the oil, stirring often, until golden brown, about 3 minutes. Stir in the garlic and cook for 1 minute to release its fragrance.

Add the garlic mixture to the chard, season to taste with salt, and stir well to coat the chard evenly. Taste and add more salt if needed.

Transfer to a serving dish. Let cool, then serve at room temperature.

Serves 4

1 large bunch green Swiss chard, about 1¼ lb (625 g)

2 tablespoons extra-virgin olive oil

2 tablespoons pine nuts

2 cloves garlic, minced

Salt

Dry-fried Green Beans

Chinese dry-fried dishes have sauces that cling like a glaze to the ingredients. During the last seconds of cooking, broth is added to the hot wok and is quickly reduced over high heat, intensifying the flavors and infusing the green beans.

Peanut oil

1 lb (500 g) green beans, trimmed and cut into 2-inch (5-cm) pieces

1 tablespoon dried baby shrimp (prawns)

1 tablespoon peeled and finely minced fresh ginger

3 cloves garlic, minced

¼ lb (125 g) ground (minced) pork butt

1 green (spring) onion, including the tender green top, chopped

1 teaspoon sugar

Large pinch of freshly ground white pepper

2 teaspoons soy sauce

2 tablespoons Chicken Stock (page 288) or broth

Asian sesame oil for drizzling

In a wok or frying pan over medium-high heat, warm 2 tablespoons peanut oil. Add one-third of the green beans, and cook, stirring occasionally, until crisp and slightly charred and blistered, about 2 minutes. Transfer to a plate and set aside. Repeat the process twice to cook the remaining beans, adding more oil as needed. (If your wok is well seasoned, you will need only 1 tablespoon of oil for each batch.)

Place the dried shrimp in a small bowl, add warm water to cover, and soak for 5 minutes. Drain and mince.

Reheat the wok over medium-high heat and add 1½ teaspoons peanut oil. Add the ginger and garlic and stir for 15 seconds. Add the pork and shrimp and stir until the mixture is crumbled and dry, about 2 minutes. Add the green onion, sugar, pepper, and soy sauce; mix thoroughly. Raise the heat to high, return the green beans to the wok, add the stock, and toss vigorously until the liquid is reduced and absorbed, about 2 minutes. Season to taste with sesame oil.

To serve, transfer the green bean mixture to a warmed serving dish and serve hot.

Serves 4–6

Creamy Tex-Mex Corn with Lime

This easy, adaptable dish is spiked with lime, cumin, and chili powder, but it can be flavored to fit many cuisines. For an Indian accent, use curry powder, lemon zest, and cilantro in place of the chili powder, lime zest and chives.

In a large, nonstick frying pan over medium heat, warm the oil. Add the corn, shallot, garlic, cumin, and chili powder and sauté until the corn starts to soften, about 4 minutes.

Stir in the milk and cheese and simmer, uncovered, until the liquid thickens, about 4 minutes. Mix in the lime zest and chives and season to taste with salt and pepper.

Transfer to a warmed serving bowl, garnish with the zest strips and snipped chives, and serve at once.

Serves 4–6

1 tablespoon olive oil

3 cups (18 oz/560 g) corn kernels

1 large shallot, chopped

1 clove garlic, chopped

1 teaspoon ground cumin

1 teaspoon chili powder

1 cup (8 fl oz/250 ml) whole milk

2 tablespoons fresh goat cheese

1 1/2 teaspoons minced lime zest, plus zest strips for garnish

1/4 cup (1/3 oz/10 g) snipped fresh chives, plus more for garnish

Salt and freshly ground pepper

Artichoke and Radicchio Barley "Risotto"

Risotto is a specialty in Northern Italy. Cook barley as you would rice for risotto and the end result is a delicious dish with some of the same chewy-creamy characteristics as the legendary Italian favorite.

Juice of 1 lemon

16 baby artichokes, about 1 lb (500 g) total weight, outer leaves removed and discarded

1 head radicchio, about ¼ lb (125 g)

1 tablespoon olive oil

¾ cup (3 oz/90 g) chopped yellow onion

1 cup (7 oz/220 g) pearl barley

3¼ cups (26 fl oz/810 ml) Vegetable Stock (page 289) or broth

2 teaspoons chopped fresh thyme, plus sprigs for garnish (optional)

2 tablespoons grated Parmesan cheese, plus more for garnish

Salt and freshly ground pepper

Fill a bowl three-fourths full of water and add the lemon juice. Cut off about 1 inch (2.5 cm) from the top of each artichoke to remove the prickly tips. Cut off the stem end. Cut the trimmed artichokes lengthwise in halves or quarters, depending upon their size, and drop into the lemon water. Meanwhile, bring a saucepan three-fourths full of water to a boil. Drain the artichokes and add them to the boiling water. Cook until tender when pierced with the tip of a sharp knife, about 10 minutes. Drain well and set aside.

Remove 6 of the outer leaves from the radicchio and set aside. Thinly slice enough radicchio to measure 1 cup (3 oz/90 g). Set aside.

In a saucepan over medium heat, warm the olive oil. Add the onion and sauté until softened, 3–4 minutes. Add the barley and stir for 1 minute. Stir in 2 cups (16 fl oz/500 ml) of the stock, bring to a simmer, and cook, stirring frequently, for 10 minutes. Add the remaining 1¼ cups (10 fl oz/310 ml) stock and continue to simmer, stirring frequently, until the barley is creamy and tender, about 15 minutes. Stir in the artichokes and chopped thyme and cook until heated through, 1–2 minutes. Remove from the heat and stir in ⅔ cup (2 oz/60 g) of the sliced radicchio and the 2 tablespoons Parmesan cheese. Season to taste with salt and pepper.

Place one of the reserved radicchio leaves in each of 6 individual bowls. Divide the barley evenly among the bowls. Sprinkle with the remaining sliced radicchio and a little Parmesan cheese. Garnish with thyme sprigs, if using. Serve at once.

Serves 6

Green Chile Nachos

An easy, flavorful appetizer for any casual event, these festive nachos are perfect for a Fourth-of-July party, thanks to the red, white, and blue colors of the dish.

Preheat the broiler (grill). Position the broiler pan about 6 inches (15 cm) from the heat source.

To make the salsa, in a bowl, combine the tomatoes, green onions, lime juice, cilantro, chiles (if using), cumin, and salt. Stir well until combined.

To make the nachos, spread the chips over the bottom of a flameproof baking dish. Sprinkle the chips evenly with the diced chiles. Sprinkle with the cheese. Using about $1/4$ cup ($1^1/2$ oz/45 g) of the salsa, put little dabs of the salsa over the cheese.

Place the dish under the broiler and heat just until the cheese melts, about 4 minutes. Watch carefully, as the cheese melts quickly.

Using pot holders, carefully remove the dish from the broiler and put it on a wire rack to cool. Let the nachos sit until they are cool enough to touch, about 3 minutes.

Put the remaining salsa in a small serving bowl. Serve the warm nachos from the baking dish or, using a spatula, transfer them to a serving plate. Serve with the salsa.

Serves 4

FOR THE SALSA:

6 small, ripe plum (Roma) tomatoes, chopped

2 green (spring) onions, white and pale green parts only, thinly sliced

Juice of 1 small lime

Leaves of 6 fresh cilantro sprigs or 2 fresh flat-leaf parsley sprigs, finely chopped

1 tablespoon well-drained canned diced green chiles (optional)

$1/2$ teaspoon ground cumin

$1/2$ teaspoon salt

FOR THE NACHOS:

4 to 5 cups blue corn tortilla chips (4–6 oz/125–185 g)

1 tablespoon well-drained canned diced green chiles

2 cups (8 oz/250 g) shredded Monterey jack cheese

Artichokes, Roman Style

Rome's *Campo de Fiori* market offers some of the world's most beautiful artichokes. The outer leaves, after being removed, can be steamed and enjoyed on their own with a dipping sauce of olive oil and lemon juice.

Fill a bowl three-fourths full of water and add the lemon juice. Working with 1 artichoke at a time, break off the tough outer leaves, until you reach the pale yellow-green inner leaves. Cut off about 1 inch (2.5 cm) from the top of the artichoke. Using a small, sharp knife, cut off the bottom of the stem and then peel the stem until it is a pale green. Drop the trimmed artichokes into the lemon water to prevent browning and put an inverted plate in the bowl to keep them fully submerged.

In a small bowl, combine the parsley, mint, garlic, 2 tablespoons of the olive oil, and a large pinch of salt and stir to mix well.

One at a time, remove the artichokes from the lemon water and, using your fingertips, gently open them slightly to expose the choke. Again using your fingers, pull out the prickly inner leaves and discard. Using a spoon, scoop out and discard the hairy chokes. Spoon one-fourth of the herb mixture into each artichoke cavity, set aside.

In a 4-qt (2-l) saucepan over medium heat, warm the remaining 2 tablespoons olive oil. Add the artichokes, stem ends up, and then add the wine and 2 tablespoons of water. Bring to a simmer, cover, and adjust the heat to maintain a gentle simmer. Cook until the artichoke bottoms are tender when pierced, about 30 minutes.

Transfer the artichokes to a platter, stem ends up. Taste the cooking liquid; add salt if needed, then reduce it over medium-high heat to about $1/4$ cup (2 fl oz/60 ml). Spoon over the artichokes. Serve warm (not hot) or at room temperature.

Serves 4

Juice of 1 lemon

4 large artichokes

2 tablespoons chopped fresh flat-leaf (Italian) parsley

2 tablespoons chopped fresh mint

2 cloves garlic, minced

4 tablespoons (2 fl oz/60 ml) olive oil

Salt

$1/2$ cup (4 fl oz/125 ml) dry white wine

Chickpeas Stewed with Chorizo

This tapa is served mostly during the winter months when heartier fare is in order. The use of cloves and cinnamon in a savory dish is reminiscent of the cooking of North Africa, just a stone's throw away from the southern tip of Spain.

2 cups (14 oz/440 g) dried chickpeas (garbanzo beans)

1/4 teaspoon ground cloves

1/4 teaspoon ground cinnamon

1 bay leaf

Large pinch of dried thyme

1/4 cup (2 fl oz/60 ml) extra-virgin olive oil

1 yellow onion, minced

4 cloves garlic, minced

3 Spanish-style chorizo sausages, about 3/4 lb (375 g) total weight, pricked with a fork

Salt and freshly ground pepper

1 1/2 teaspoons chopped fresh flat-leaf (Italian) parsley

Pick over the chickpeas and discard any misshapen peas or stones. Rinse and drain. Place the chickpeas in a bowl, add cold water to cover generously, and let soak for at least 4 hours or up to overnight.

Drain the chickpeas and place in a saucepan with the cloves, cinnamon, bay leaf, thyme, and water to cover by 2 inches (5 cm). Bring to a boil over high heat, reduce the heat to low, and simmer, uncovered, until the skins just begin to crack and the chickpeas are tender, 45–60 minutes. Remove from the heat and set aside.

In a large frying pan over medium heat, warm the olive oil. Add the onion, garlic, and chorizo and cook, stirring, until the onion is soft, about 10 minutes. Add the chickpeas and their liquid and simmer slowly, uncovered, stirring occasionally, until the liquid is almost evaporated, about 40 minutes. Season with salt and pepper to taste.

Carefully transfer the chorizo to a cutting board. Slice it on the diagonal into slices about 1/4 (6 mm) inch thick. Return the chorizo slices to the pan and cook until heated through, about 1 minute.

To serve, transfer the chickpeas and chorizo to a warmed serving dish. Garnish with the parsley and serve immediately.

Serves 6

Onion and Olive Tart

Make the tart dough and refrigerate it for at least 1 hour or up to 3 days.

To make the tapanade, in a food processor, combine the olives, capers, anchovies, garlic, lemon zest, pepper, and 2 tablespoons of the olive oil. Pulse to form a coarse purée, adding more oil if needed to achieve a spreadable consistency. Set aside.

In a large sauté pan over medium heat, melt the butter with the olive oil. Add the onions and sauté, stirring occasionally, until very soft, about 20 minutes. Sprinkle with the flour, and salt and pepper to taste, and continue to cook, stirring, for 2 minutes longer. Add the thyme and stir briefly, then remove from the heat and let cool for 10 minutes. Meanwhile, in a small bowl, whisk together the cream and eggs. Season with salt and pepper.

Preheat the oven to 425°F (220°C). On a lightly floured work surface, roll out the tart dough into a round 11-inches (28-cm) in diameter. Carefully transfer the dough to a 9-inch (23-cm) fluted tart pan with a removable bottom. Fit the dough in the pan and cutt off the excess dough even with the rim. Line the tart shell with aluminum foil and fill with pie weights. Bake until the crust is slightly set, 10–15 minutes. Remove from the oven and remove the weights and foil. Let cool for 10 minutes. Reduce the oven temperature to 350°F (180°C).

Spread the tapenade in the cooled tart shell. Top with the onion mixture, spreading it evenly. Pour in the egg mixture and top with the cheese. Bake until the filling is set, about 25 minutes.

Let the tart cool on a wire rack for 10 minutes, then transfer to a serving plate. Cut into wedges and serve warm or at room temperature.

Makes one 9-inch (23-cm) tart, Serves 8

1 Basic Tart Dough (page 291)

FOR THE TAPENADE:

1/2 cup (2 1/2 oz/75 g) pitted Niçoise or Kalamata olives

1 tablespoon capers, rinsed

2 teaspoons chopped anchovy fillets

1 teaspoon minced garlic

1 teaspoon grated lemon zest

1/2 teaspoon freshly ground pepper

2–3 tablespoons extra-virgin olive oil

3 tablespoons unsalted butter

1 tablespoon olive oil

3 large yellow onions, cut into slices 1/4 inch (6 mm) thick

2 tablespoons all-purpose (plain) flour

Salt and freshly ground pepper

2 teaspoons chopped fresh thyme

1 cup (8 fl oz/250 ml) heavy (double) cream

2 eggs

1/2 cup (2 oz/60 g) shredded Gruyère or Emmentaler cheese

Green Beans Stewed with Tomatoes and Garlic

Fresh green beans that are just past their prime will work well for this dish. If you like, you may substitute ½ of the green beans for yellow wax beans for extra color. Pair this dish with a hearty meat such as lamb and some rice pilaf.

2 tablespoons olive oil

1 small yellow onion, chopped

4 cloves garlic, thinly sliced

1 lb (500 g) green beans, trimmed

2 cups (12 oz/375 g) peeled, seeded, and chopped fresh or canned tomatoes

2 tablespoons chopped fresh flat-leaf (Italian) parsley

Salt and freshly ground pepper

In a large frying pan over medium heat, warm the olive oil. Add the onion and cook, stirring occasionally, until soft, about 7 minutes. Add the garlic and stir for 1 minute to release its fragrance.

Raise the heat to high and add the beans, tomatoes, and parsley. Bring to a simmer, reduce the heat to low, cover, and cook until the beans are very tender and soft, about 30 minutes.

Uncover, raise the heat to medium, and continue to cook until most of the liquid has evaporated, about 10 minutes longer. Season to taste with salt and pepper.

Transfer to a serving plate and serve hot or at room temperature.

Serves 6

Breakfast & Brunch

Buttermilk Pancakes with Bing Cherry Syrup

FOR THE BING CHERRY SYRUP:

¹/₂ cup (3¹/₂ oz/105 g) firmly packed golden brown sugar

¹/₂ cup (4 oz/125 g) granulated sugar

1¹/₄ cups (9 oz/280 g) stemmed and pitted large Bing cherries

1 teaspoon almond extract (essence)

FOR THE PANCAKES:

2 eggs

2 cups (10 oz/315 g) all-purpose (plain) flour

2 tablespoons granulated sugar

2 teaspoons baking powder

1 teaspoon baking soda (bicarbonate of soda)

1 teaspoon salt

2 cups (16 fl oz/500 ml) buttermilk

¹/₄ cup (2 oz/60 g) unsalted butter, melted

¹/₂ teaspoon almond extract (essence)

1–2 tablespoons vegetable oil

To make the syrup, in a saucepan over high heat, combine the brown and granulated sugars and 1 cup (8 fl oz/250 ml) warm water and stir until the sugar dissolves. Bring to a boil and cook, uncovered, for 5 minutes. Add the cherries, reduce the heat to low, and simmer until the cherries are tender, 8–10 minutes. Stir in the almond extract and simmer for about 2 minutes longer to blend the flavors. Remove from the heat and let cool.

To make pancakes, in a small bowl, using an electric mixer, beat the eggs until frothy. Add the flour, granulated sugar, baking powder, baking soda, salt, buttermilk, melted butter, and almond extract. Continue to beat just until the mixture is smooth; do not overbeat.

Preheat the oven to 200°F (95°C).

Heat a large, heavy frying pan or griddle over medium heat until a few drops of water flicked onto the surface skitter across it. Brush the pan lightly with the vegetable oil. Pour three, ¹/₄ cup (2 fl oz/60 ml) measurements of the batter onto the pan. Cook until small bubbles appear on the surfaces, the batter is set, the bottoms are lightly browned, and the edges look dry, about 2 minutes. Using a spatula, flip the pancakes over and continue to cook until the second side is golden brown, about 2 minutes longer. Transfer to a baking sheet and place in the warm oven until all of the pancakes are cooked. Repeat with the remaining batter, adding more oil to the pan as needed.

Serve the pancakes hot, topped with a large spoonful of the cherry syrup.

Makes twelve 6-inch (15-cm) pancakes; serves 4

Black and White Doughnut Holes

For light-as-a-feather doughnut holes, keep all the ingredients as cold as possible before frying them. If you decide to make doughnuts rather than just the holes, cook them for 5–7 minutes. This recipe will make about 3 dozen doughnuts.

Sift the 3$^{1}/_{2}$ cups flour into a large bowl. Then sift the flour again with the baking powder, baking soda, nutmeg, mace, cardamom, and salt. Set aside. In a bowl, using an electric mixer set on medium speed, beat the eggs until frothy. Gradually add the granulated sugar, beating until the mixture is light and lemon colored, about 4 minutes. Add the buttermilk, melted butter, and lemon extract and mix well. Pour the egg mixture into the center of the flour mixture and mix thoroughly. The dough will be very soft; add an additional sprinkle of flour if necessary. Dust a work surface generously with more flour. Scrape the dough onto the surface and dust the top with flour. Roll out the dough about $^{1}/_{3}$ inch (9 mm) thick. Dip the center removable part of a doughnut cutter into a side dish of extra flour and cut out holes. Using an icing spatula, lift the holes onto an ungreased baking sheet. Cover with plastic wrap and refrigerate for at least 2 hours or up to 1 day.

To fry the doughnuts, in a deep saucepan, pour in oil to a depth of 3 inches (7.5 cm) and heat to 380°F (193°C) on a deep-frying thermometer. Working in small batches, slip the doughnut holes into the oil and fry until golden brown, about 2 minutes. Using a skimmer or slotted spoon, transfer to paper towels to drain.

Sift 1 cup (4 oz/125 g) of the confectioners' sugar into a paper bag. Sift together the remaining $^{1}/_{2}$ cup (2 oz/60 g) confectioners' sugar with the cocoa into another bag. Just before serving, shake half of the doughnut holes in the bag with the plain sugar and the other half with the cocoa-sugar mixture. Serve immediately.

Makes 9 dozen doughnut holes

3$^{1}/_{2}$ cups (17$^{1}/_{2}$ oz/545 g) all-purpose (plain) flour, plus more as needed

1$^{1}/_{2}$ teaspoons baking powder

$^{1}/_{2}$ teaspoon baking soda (bicarbonate of soda)

$^{1}/_{4}$ teaspoon ground nutmeg

Pinch of ground mace

Pinch of ground cardamom

Pinch of salt

2 eggs

1 cup (8 oz/250 g) granulated sugar

1 cup (8 fl oz/250 ml) buttermilk

2 tablespoons unsalted butter, melted and slightly cooled

1 teaspoon lemon extract (essence)

Vegetable oil for deep-frying

1$^{1}/_{2}$ cups (6 oz/185 g) confectioners' (icing) sugar

$^{1}/_{2}$ cup (1$^{1}/_{2}$ oz/45 g) Dutch-process cocoa powder

Eggs Benedict

This well-known brunch dish never goes out of style. When tomatoes are in season, consider topping the ham with a broiled tomato slice before crowning it with the egg and the hollandaise. Or, try substituting sautéed fresh spinach for the ham.

FOR THE HOLLANDAISE SAUCE:

4 egg yolks

3¹/2 tablespoons *each* fresh lemon and lime juice

Salt

2 pinches of freshly ground white pepper

Pinch of cayenne pepper

1 cup (8 oz/250 g) unsalted butter, melted and slightly cooled

4 English muffins, split

3 teaspoons unsalted butter

8 slices baked ham, each ¹/4 inch (6 mm) thick and cut to fit the muffins

8 eggs, poached (see page 291)

Preheat the broiler (grill). Meanwhile, make the hollandaise sauce: In a small, heavy saucepan over very low heat, combine the egg yolks, lemon and lime juices, and 1 tablespoon water. Whisk until the mixture just begins to thicken. Scrape the yolk mixture into a blender, add ¹/8 teaspoon salt and the white and cayenne peppers, and blend until smooth. Let cool for 1 minute. With the motor running, slowly pour in the melted butter in a thin stream until all of it has been incorporated. Taste and adjust the seasonings. Pour the sauce into a bowl and place over (not touching) hot water in a saucepan. Keep warm until serving.

Lightly spread the cut sides of the muffins with 2 teaspoons of the butter and place on a broiler pan. Broil (grill) until brown, about 6 minutes. Turn off the broiler, cover the muffins with aluminum foil, and keep warm in the oven.

Meanwhile, in a small sauté pan over medium-high heat, melt the remaining 1 teaspoon butter. Add the ham and cook, turning once, until it is beginning to brown, about 4 minutes total. Transfer the ham to a baking sheet and keep warm in the oven.

For each portion, place a muffin half on a plate. Top with a slice of ham and then an egg. Spoon the sauce evenly over the tops. Serve at once.

Serves 8

Cinnamon French Toast with Sautéed Bananas, Pecans, and Maple Syrup

Fuel up for a day of skiing or other winter sports with this cinnamon-scented French toast. Pan-fried bacon or sausage links would make fine accompaniments. If you like, you can substitute walnut halves or slivered almonds for the pecans.

Preheat the oven to 350°F (180°C). Spread the pecans on a baking sheet and toast in the oven until golden and fragrant, 5–8 minutes. Transfer to a plate. Reduce the oven temperature to 250°F (120°C).

In a bowl, whisk together the eggs, milk, and 1 teaspoon cinnamon until blended. Pour into a large, shallow glass or ceramic dish. Working in batches, add enough bread slices to fit the pan comfortably. Soak the slices, turning once, for a few seconds total. Carefully transfer the slices to a plate and repeat until all the slices are soaked.

Have ready a baking sheet. In a large, heavy frying pan or griddle over high heat, warm ½ tablespoon each of butter and vegetable oil. When hot, add enough bread slices to fit comfortably in a single layer and cook until golden brown on the first side, about 2 minutes. Turn and cook until golden on the second side, about 2 minutes longer. Transfer to the baking sheet and place in the warm oven. Repeat until all the soaked bread is cooked, adding more butter and oil in equal amounts as needed.

To make the topping, in a large, heavy frying pan over medium-high heat, melt the butter. Add the sliced bananas and sauté, stirring constantly, until warm, about 1 minute. Remove from the heat.

To serve, place 2 toasts on each warmed individual plate. Top with the sautéed bananas, dividing evenly. Sprinkle each serving with some cinnamon and toasted nuts, then drizzle with maple syrup. Pass the remaining syrup at the table.

Serves 4

⅓ cup (1½ oz/45 g) pecan halves

4 eggs

1 cup (8 fl oz/250 ml) whole milk

1 teaspoon ground cinnamon, plus more for sprinkling

8 slices good-quality day-old white bread, each about ½ inch (12 mm) thick

Unsalted butter

Vegetable oil

FOR THE TOPPING:

1½ tablespoons unsalted butter

3 large, ripe bananas, peeled and cut into slices ¼ inch (6 mm) thick

1 cup (11 fl oz/345 ml) pure maple syrup, heated

English Scones

Serve these fine-textured scones with strawberry jam or softened butter. If you like, add ½ cup (3 oz/90 g) chopped plumped dried apricots, whole raisins, or fresh berries to the dough just before it is kneaded.

2 cups (10 oz/315 g) all-purpose (plain) flour, plus flour for dusting

2 teaspoons cream of tartar

1 teaspoon baking soda (bicarbonate of soda)

1 teaspoon sugar

½ teaspoon salt

4 tablespoons (2 oz/60 g) unsalted butter, chilled and cut into pieces

¾ cup (6 fl oz/180 ml) whole milk

Preheat the oven to 450°F (230°C). Lightly grease a baking sheet.

In a food processor, combine the flour, cream of tartar, baking soda, sugar, and salt. Pulse to combine. Add the butter and process using on-off pulses until the mixture resembles coarse meal. Transfer to a bowl. (Alternatively, in a bowl, stir together the dry ingredients. Then, using a pastry blender, cut in the butter until the mixture resembles coarse meal.)

Make a well in the center of the flour mixture and pour in the milk. Using a fork, mix the ingredients together just until a soft elastic dough forms.

Turn out the dough onto a lightly floured work surface and knead 5 or 6 times until the dough is smooth. Roll out the dough about ¾ inch (2 cm) thick. Using a scallop-edged cookie cutter 3 inches (7.5 cm) in diameter, cut out 8–10 rounds. Transfer the dough rounds to the prepared baking sheet.

Bake the scones until they rise and are golden brown on top, about 10 minutes. Serve hot.

Makes 8–10 scones

Stuffed French Toast Grand Marnier

To make the orange butter, in a small bowl or a food processor, combine the butter, orange zest, and liqueur and beat or process until smooth. Transfer to a small serving bowl or individual crocks and refrigerate until serving.

Preheat the oven to 200°F (95°C). To make the filling, in a small, nonreactive saucepan over medium heat, combine the cherries, apricots, orange zest, juice, and liqueur. Bring to a simmer, and remove from the heat. Stir in the cinnamon, cover, and let stand for 10 minutes. Stir in the banana slices.

Using a small, sharp knife, cut a narrow horizontal pocket in the center of one side of each bread slice, keeping three sides intact. Spoon about 1 1/2 tablespoons of the fruit filling into each pocket, then press the top with the palm of your hand to seal. Set aside.

In a shallow bowl, whisk the eggs until frothy. Whisk in the milk, liqueur, brown sugar, and salt. Dip the filled bread slices into the egg mixture and let soak, turning once, for about 2 minutes on each side.

Heat a large, heavy frying pan or griddle over high heat until a few drops of water flicked onto the surface skitter across it. Add about 1 tablespoon of the butter and, when the foam subsides, working in batches, add the French toast. Cook until golden brown on one side, about 3 minutes. Turn and brown the other side, about 2 minutes longer. Transfer to a heatproof platter and place in the warm oven. Repeat until all the French toast is cooked, adding more butter to the pan as needed.

Divide the French toast among warmed individual plates and serve with the orange butter.

Serves 6

FOR THE ORANGE BUTTER:

1 cup (8oz/250 g) unsalted butter, at room temperature

Grated zest of 1 orange

1 teaspoon Grand Marnier

FOR THE FILLING:

1/4 cup (1 1/2 oz/45 g) dried cherries

1/4 cup (1 1/2 oz/45 g) dried apricots, slivered

Grated zest of 1/2 orange

1/4 cup (2 fl oz/60 ml) orange juice

2 tablespoons Grand Marnier

1/2 teaspoon ground cinnamon

1/2 large ripe banana, thinly sliced

12 slices challah bread, each 2 inches (5 cm) thick

4 eggs

1 cup (8 fl oz/250 ml) whole milk

1/4 cup (2 fl oz/60 ml) Grand Marnier

2 tablespoons firmly packed light brown sugar

Pinch of salt

About 2 tablespoons unsalted butter

Oven-Baked Omelet with Sausage and Peppers

FOR THE FILLING:

10 oz (315 g) Italian sausages

1/2 head garlic, unpeeled, plus 4 cloves

1 1/2 cups (12 fl oz/375 ml) dry red wine

2 tablespoons olive oil

1 leek, 2 inches (4 cm) long, white part only, julienned

1/2 *each* yellow bell pepper (capsicum) and red bell pepper (capsicum), seeded and cut lengthwise into strips

1 green bell pepper (capsicum), seeded and cut lengthwise into strips

1 teaspoon minced fresh oregano

Salt and freshly ground pepper

5–6 tablespoons (2 1/2–3 oz/ 75–90 g) unsalted butter

9 eggs, separated

1/4 cup (1 1/2 oz/45 g) all-purpose (plain) flour

1/2 cup (4 fl oz/125 ml) heavy (double) cream

Pinch of cayenne pepper

1/2 cup (2 oz/60 g) grated Parmesan cheese

To make the filling, in a large saucepan over medium-high heat, combine the sausages and 1/2 head garlic with enough cold water to cover by 1 inch (2.5 cm). Cover, bring to a boil, reduce the heat to low, and simmer until the fat spurts out when the sausages are pierced with a fork, about 25 minutes. Drain the sausages, cut into slices 1/4 inch (6 mm) thick, and return to a cleanpan. Add the 4 garlic cloves and the red wine. Bring to a boil, reduce the heat to low, cover partially, and cook until the wine is absorbed, about 45 minutes. Remove from the heat.

In a large sauté pan over medium-high heat, warm the olive oil. Add the leek and sauté until it begins to soften, about 5 minutes. Stir in the bell peppers and continue to sauté until the vegetables are tender, about 10 minutes. Add the oregano and salt and pepper to taste. Add the sausages and stir to mix well. Taste, and adjust the seasonings.

Preheat the oven to 400°F (200°C). Place the butter in a 10-inch (25-cm) baking dish and put it in the oven until it melts and becomes nutty brown, about 5 minutes.

Meanwhile, in a bowl, using an electric mixer, beat the egg whites and a pinch of salt until stiff peaks form. In another bowl, beat the egg yolks until thick. Add the flour, cream, cayenne, and 1/4 teaspoon black pepper to the yolks and mix well. Using a rubber spatula, fold in the whites.

Remove the dish from the oven. Pour half of the egg mixture into the hot pan, scatter the sausage filling on top, then top with the remaining egg mixture. Sprinkle with the Parmesan cheese, and return to the oven. Bake for 5 minutes. Reduce the oven temperature to 350°F (180°C) and continue to bake until light brown on top and firm when pressed with a finger, 15–17 minutes.

Serve the omelet directly from the dish.

Serves 6

Roast Beef Hash

The combination of marjoram and rosemary lends an herbal note to this classic, well-loved breakfast dish. While it bakes unattended in the oven, you're free to visit with your guests. For a classic presentation, top each serving with a poached egg.

Preheat the oven to 375°F (190°C).

In a heavy, ovenproof frying pan, preferably cast-iron, melt the butter over medium heat. When the foam subsides, add the onions and sauté until they begin to soften, about 3 minutes. Add the potatoes and 2–3 tablespoons oil if needed to prevent sticking, and fry, turning often with a spatula, until browned, about 8 minutes. Add the roast beef and fry, stirring often, until lightly browned, 3–4 minutes. Add the ¼ cup parsley, the rosemary, and marjoram and season to taste with salt and pepper. Mix well. Taste, and adjust the seasonings. Pour in the milk and bring to a boil.

Transfer the pan to the oven and bake, uncovered, until the potatoes are browned and tender, about 30 minutes. Serve hot, garnished with parsley, directly from the pan, or transfer to a warmed serving dish.

Serves 6

3 tablespoons unsalted butter

3 large yellow onions, chopped

3 large baking potatoes, peeled and chopped

Vegetable oil

About 2½ lb (1.25 kg) cooked roast beef, cut into large cubes

¼ cup (⅓ oz/10 g) chopped fresh flat-leaf (Italian) parsley, plus more for garnish

1 tablespoon chopped fresh rosemary leaves

1 tablespoon chopped fresh marjoram leaves

Salt and freshly ground pepper

1 cup (8 fl oz/250 ml) whole milk

Pepper Jack Pancakes with Tomato Salsa

FOR THE SALSA:

6 ripe plum (Roma) tomatoes, halved, seeded, and cut into 1/2-inch (12-mm) dice

2/3 cup (2 oz/60 g) chopped green (spring) onions, including 2 inches (5 cm) of the green tops

2 jalapeño chiles, finely diced

2 tablespoons chopped fresh cilantro (fresh coriander)

2 tablespoons lime juice

About 1/2 teaspoon salt

FOR THE PANCAKES:

2 cups (10 oz/315 g) yellow cornmeal

1 cup (5 oz/155 g) all-purpose (plain) flour

1 tablespoon baking powder

1 teaspoon salt

2/3 cup (2 1/2 oz/75 g) finely shredded pepper jack cheese

About 2 1/2 cups (20 fl oz/ 625 ml) milk

4 eggs, lightly beaten

1/4 cup (2 oz/60 g) unsalted butter, melted and cooled

2–3 tablespoons vegetable oil

6 tablespoons (3 fl oz/90 ml) sour cream

To make the salsa, in a bowl, stir together the tomatoes, green onions, chiles, cilantro, lime juice, and 1/2 teaspoon salt. Taste and add more salt, if needed. You should have about 3 cups (24 fl oz/750 ml) salsa. Set aside.

Preheat the oven to 200°F (95°C). Have ready 2 baking sheets and aluminum foil.

To make the pancakes, in large bowl, whisk together the cornmeal, flour, baking powder, and salt. Add the cheese and toss to mix. In another bowl, whisk together 2 cups (16 fl oz/500 ml) of the milk, the eggs, and melted butter. Pour the milk mixture over the flour mixture and stir until just combined. The batter should be thick, yet still pourable; if needed, stir in up to 1/2 cup (4 fl oz/125 ml) more milk to achieve the desired consistency.

Heat a griddle or large, heavy frying pan over medium heat. Brush the pan lightly with some of the oil. Using a 1/4 cup (2-fl oz/60-ml) measure, ladle the batter onto the griddle; try to leave about 1/2-inch between each pancake. Cook until small bubbles appear on the surfaces and the bottoms are lightly browned, about 1 1/2 minutes. Using a spatula, flip the pancakes over and cook until the second sides are lightly browned and the pancakes are just cooked through, 1–2 minutes longer. Transfer them to a baking sheet in one layer, tent loosely with aluminum foil, and place in the warm oven. Repeat, using more oil as needed, until all the batter is used. You should have about 18 pancakes.

To serve, place 3 pancakes on each warmed individual plate. Spoon about 1/3 cup (3 fl oz/80 ml) salsa onto each serving and top each with about 1 tablespoon sour cream. Pass the remaining salsa at the table.

Serves 6

Shrimp Gratin

Peel and devein the shrimp. Meanwhile, bring a saucepan three-fourths full of water to a boil over high heat. Add the shrimp and cook just until they curl slightly and are firm, about 2 minutes. Drain well and set aside.

Preheat the oven to 375°F (190°C). Butter a shallow 4-qt (4-l) baking dish.

In a large sauté pan over medium-high heat, warm the olive oil. Add 1 cup (5 oz/55 g) of the onions and the fennel and sauté until soft and translucent, about 5 minutes. Add the shrimp and sauté for 1 minute. Raise the heat to high, pour in the Pernod, and cook, stirring constantly, until all the liquid evaporates, about 3 minutes. Stir in the cream and tomato paste and cook until bubbly, about 2 minutes. Add ¹/₂ cup (²/₃ oz/20 g) of the dill, the parsley, and season to taste with salt and black pepper, and mix well. Transfer to the prepared baking dish and set aside.

In a saucepan over medium heat, bring the milk almost to a boil. Shred the cheese and set aside. In a heavy saucepan over medium heat, melt the ¹/₄ cup (2 oz/60 g) butter. Add the remaining onions and sauté until translucent, about 5 minutes. Add the flour, raise the heat to medium-high, and cook, stirring constantly, for 2 minutes, adjusting the heat if the flour begins to brown. Remove from the heat. Add the hot milk all at once and whisk vigorously to prevent lumps from forming. Return the pan to medium heat and cook, stirring constantly, until thickened, about 2 minutes. Season with the remaining dill, salt to taste, and cayenne pepper. Add half of the cheese and stir until the cheese melts. Slowly whisk in the wine, adding enough to thin the sauce to a thick and creamy consistency. Pour the cream sauce over the shrimp mixture, covering it completely. Sprinkle with the crushed corn flakes, then dot with the 1 tablespoon butter. Bake until browned and bubbly, about 30 minutes. Serve hot directly from the dish.

Serves 8

3 lb (1.5 kg) shrimp (prawns)

2 tablespoons olive oil

3 cups chopped yellow onions

1 fennel bulb, thinly sliced

¹/₄ cup (2 fl oz/60 ml) Pernod

3 tablespoons heavy (double) cream

2 tablespoons tomato paste

³/₄ cup (1 oz/30 g) chopped fresh dill

¹/₄ cup (¹/₃ oz/10 g) chopped fresh flat-leaf (Italian) parsley

Salt and freshly ground black pepper

1¹/₂ cups (12 fl oz/375 ml) milk

6 oz (185 g) Swiss cheese

¹/₄ cup (2 oz/60 g) unsalted butter, plus 1 tablespoon

¹/₂ cup (2¹/₂ oz/75 g) all-purpose (plain) flour

Pinch of cayenne pepper

1–1¹/₃ cups (8–11 fl oz/ 250–330 ml) dry white wine

¹/₂ cup (¹/₂ oz/15 g) corn flakes, crushed

Eggs with Sweet Peppers, Tomato, and Ham

In a small frying pan over medium heat, warm the olive oil. Add the green onions and garlic and sauté for about 1 minute to soften them and release their fragrance. Add the bell pepper, cover, and reduce the heat to medium-low. Cook until the pepper is tender, 12–15 minutes.

Add the tomatoes and bay leaf, season to taste with salt and pepper, and cook uncovered, stirring often, until the mixture is thick, about 5 minutes. Add a little water if the mixture gets too thick. Remove the bay leaf and discard.

While the sauce simmers, in an 8-inch (20-cm) nonstick frying pan over medium heat, melt the butter. Cut the ham into 4 equal pieces, add to the hot frying pan, and sauté, turning once, until lightly browned, about 1 minute on each side. Transfer to a plate and keep warm.

Add the eggs to the tomato sauce and season to taste with salt and pepper. Cook over medium-low heat, stirring constantly and scraping the sides and bottom of the pan with a heatproof rubber spatula, until the mixture is thick, about 5 minutes. The eggs will not form large curds but will gradually set into a smooth, creamy, tomatoey mass.

Spoon the eggs into individual bowls and put the ham on top. Serve at once.

Serves 4

3 tablespoons olive oil

6 green (spring) onions, white and pale green parts only, minced

3 clove garlic, minced

1 green bell pepper (capsicum), seeded and thinly sliced

2 cups (12 oz/370 g) grated plum (Roma) tomatoes

1 small bay leaf

Salt and freshly ground pepper

1 tablespoon unsalted butter

4 large, thin slices cooked ham, 2–3 oz (60–90 g) each

12 eggs, lightly beaten

Dilled Batter Muffins

There's nothing like the smell of baking fresh bread or rolls in the morning, and your guests will feel extra special eating them. Rolling these moist miniature muffins in salted dill seeds gives them a crunchy coating and an extra dose of lively flavor.

3/4 cup (4 oz/120 g) all-purpose (plain) flour, plus 1 1/2 cups (6 oz/185 g) sifted flour

2 tablespoons sugar

1 tablespoon grated yellow onion

1 tablespoon dill seeds

1 package (2 1/2 teaspoons) active dry yeast

1 teaspoon salt

1/4 teaspoon baking soda (bicarbonate of soda)

2 tablespoons unsalted butter

1 cup (8 oz/250 g) small-curd cottage cheese, at room temperature

1 egg, beaten

FOR THE COATING:

1/2 cup (4 oz/125 g) unsalted butter, melted

1/2 cup (2 oz/60 g) coarse salt

Large pinch dill seeds

In the bowl of a stand mixer, stir together 1/4 cup (1 1/2 oz/45 g) of the flour, the sugar, onion, dill seeds, yeast, salt, and baking soda. In a small saucepan over low heat, warm 1/4 cup (2 fl oz/60 ml) water with the butter until it reads 130°F (54°C) on an instant-read thermometer. Add the butter mixture to the flour mixture and, using the paddle attachment, beat until smooth, about 2 minutes.

Add the cottage cheese, egg, and the remaining 1/2 cup (2 1/2 oz/75 g) flour to the mixer. Beat on high speed until smooth and elastic, about 2 minutes. Add the 1 1/2 cups (6 oz/185 g) sifted flour and again beat until smooth. Cover with plastic wrap and let rise in a warm place until doubled in bulk, about 45 minutes.

Generously grease 24 mini-muffin cups with solid vegetable shortening or nonstick cooking spray. Using a wooden spoon, stir the batter 25 times (it will deflate), then spoon it into the prepared muffin cups, dividing evenly. Cover the muffins with a damp kitchen towel and let rise until doubled in bulk, about 30 minutes. Preheat the oven to 350°F (180°C).

Bake until the muffins are puffed and brown, 20–25 minutes. Meanwhile, make the coating: Put the melted butter in a bowl. On a small plate, stir together the salt and dill seeds.

When the muffins are ready, remove from the oven and immediately turn them out onto wire racks. Roll each hot muffin first in the melted butter, then dip the tops in the salt-dill mixture. Serve at once.

Makes 24 mini muffins

Make-Ahead Eggnog French Toast

The perfect dish to have on hand for weekend guests during the holidays, this dish is made up to one week before serving and then put in the freezer. Just pop it into an oven on the morning of your party and enjoy.

Brush a baking sheet with oil and set it aside.

In a shallow bowl, combine the eggs, eggnog, sugar, vanilla, nutmeg, and salt. Beat with a fork until well blended. Dip 1 slice of the bread in the egg mixture and let it soak for about 1 minute. Using the fork, turn the bread over and let the second side soak until saturated. Put the egg-soaked bread on the prepared baking sheet. Repeat to soak the remaining bread, arranging it on the sheet in a single layer. Cover the baking sheet with foil and put it in the freezer until the bread is completely frozen. Stack the frozen slices together, slipping a square of waxed paper between each one. Wrap the stack in foil and freeze for up to 1 week.

To bake, position the oven rack in the center of the oven without another rack above it and preheat it to 425°F (220°C). In a small saucepan over low heat, melt the $1/4$ cup butter.

Remove the bread from the freezer. Unwrap the bread and using a pastry brush, brush one side of each piece of bread with the melted butter. Place the bread, buttered side down, in a single layer on an ungreased baking sheet. Place the baking sheet in the oven for 10 minutes. Remove the baking sheet from the oven. Brush the remaining butter evenly over the tops of the toast slices. Turn the toast over and return to the oven. Continue to bake until the toast is golden brown, 5–10 minutes.

Remove the baking sheet from the oven and let the french toast cool slightly. Transfer to warmed individual plates. Serve with butter and the syrup on the side.

Serves 4

Vegetable oil

3 eggs, lightly beaten

1 cup (8 fl oz/250 ml) eggnog

2 teaspoons sugar

1/2 teaspoon vanilla extract

1/8 teaspoon freshly grated nutmeg

Pinch of salt

8 slices white or whole-wheat bread

1/4 cup (2 oz/60 g) unsalted butter, plus more for serving

1/2 cup (51/2 fl oz/170 ml) maple syrup, warmed

Old-Fashioned Pecan Sticky Buns

2 packages (5 teaspoons) active dry yeast

1 teaspoon granulated sugar, plus 1/2 cup (4 oz/125 g)

8 cups (2 1/2 lb/1.25 kg) all-purpose (plain) flour

1 tablespoon salt

2 tablespoons unsalted butter, melted and cooled

2 eggs, lightly beaten

FOR THE GLAZE:

1/2 cup (4 oz/125 g) unsalted butter

2 1/4 cups (1 lb/500 g) firmly packed golden brown sugar

2 tablespoons dark corn syrup

Pinch of salt

1/2 teaspoon vanilla extract (essence)

1/3–1/2 cup (3–4 fl oz/ 80–125 ml) heavy (double) cream

Vegetable shortening (vegetable lard)

1/2 cup (4 oz/126 g) unsalted butter, melted

2 1/2 cups (10 oz/315 g) coarsely chopped pecans, toasted

In a small bowl, sprinkle the yeast over 1/4 cup (2 fl oz/60 ml) lukewarm water. Stir in the 1 teaspoon sugar and let stand until foamy, about 5 minutes. In the bowl of a stand mixture, combine 2 cups (16 fl oz/500 ml) lukewarm water, the 1/2 cup (4 oz/125 g) sugar, and 4 cups (1 1/4 lb/625 g) of the flour. Beat with the whisk attachment until smooth, about 5 minutes. Add the yeast mixture and beat for about 2 minutes. Add the salt, melted butter, eggs, and the remaining 4 cups (1 1/4 lb/625 g) flour and beat until elastic, 6–8 minutes. The dough will be sticky. Transfer to am oiled bowl and cover with plastic. Refrigerate overnight.

The next day, make the glaze: In a small saucepan over medium heat, melt the butter and stir in 1 cup (7 oz/220 g) of the brown sugar, the corn syrup, and the salt until the sugar dissolves, about 3 minutes. Remove from the heat and stir in the vanilla. In a small bowl, stir together the remaining 1 1/4 cups (9 oz/280 g) brown sugar and enough cream to form a spreadable mixture.

Grease 2 or 3 rimmed baking sheets with shortening. Spread the glaze evenly over each of the prepared pans, then scatter 2 tablespoons of the pecans over each pan. Divide the dough in half. On a floured work surface, roll out one-half of the dough into a 12-by-15-inch (30-by-38-cm) rectangle. Brush the top with the melted butter. Spread on half of the cream-sugar mixture and sprinkle with half of the remaining pecans. Beginning with a long side, roll up the dough and pinch the seam securely closed. Cut into slices 1 inch (2.5 cm) thick and arrange, cut sides down, on the prepared baking pans. Lightly cover with dampened kitchen towels and let rise until doubled, 45–50 minutes. Preheat the oven to 400°F (200°C). Bake for 10 minutes, then reduce the temperature to 350°F (180°C). Bake until the buns are browned, 20–25 minutes longer. Invert the pans onto racks, let stand for 5 minutes, then lift off the pans. Let cool for 15 minutes before serving.

Makes 2 1/2 dozen buns

Leek, Artichoke, and Chard Tart

Preheat the oven to 350°F (180°C). On a lightly floured work surface, roll out the tart dough into a round 12 inches (30 cm) in diameter. Carefully transfer the dough to a 10-inch (25-cm) fluted tart pan with a removable bottom. Fit the dough in the pan and trim off any excess dough. Line the tart shell with parchment (baking) paper and fill with pie weights. Bake until the crust is firm and lightly colored, about 15 minutes. Remove the weights and paper and let the crust cool slightly.

Meanwhile, make the filling: Fill a bowl three-fourths full of water and add the lemon juice. Working with one artichoke at a time, break off the tough outer leaves. Cut off about 1 inch (2.5 cm) from the top of each artichoke. Cut off the bottom of the stem, and peel the stem until it is pale green. Drop the trimmed artichokes into the lemon water to prevent browning. Bring a saucepan three-fourths full of salted water to a boil over high heat. Drain the artichokes, add to the boiling water, and cook until tender, 12–15 minutes. Drain, let cool slightly, then spread the artichoke centers slightly and use a spoon to scrape out the chokes. Chop the artichokes; you should have about 1 cup (6 oz/185 g).

In a large sauté pan over medium heat, warm the olive oil. Add the leeks and sauté until softened, 4–5 minutes. Add the stock, bring to a boil, and add the chopped artichokes and chard. Cover and cook until the chard is wilted, 3–5 minutes. Season to taste with salt and pepper. Let cool.

In a bowl, beat together the milk, eggs, and coriander. Stir into the cooled vegetable mixture, then, pour into the prebaked shell.

Bake until the filling is partially set, about 20 minutes. Sprinkle with the bread crumbs and dot with the cheese. Continue baking until a knife inserted in the center comes out clean, 10–15 minutes. Let stand for 15 minutes, then serve warm.

Makes one 10-inch (25-cm) tart; serves 8

Basic Tart Dough (page 291)

FOR THE FILLING:

Juice of 1 lemon

2 artichokes

3 tablespoons olive oil

2 leeks, white parts only, thinly sliced crosswise

1 cup (8 fl oz/250 ml) Vegetable Stock (page 289) or broth

2 cups (4 oz/125 g) shredded red Swiss chard leaves

Salt and freshly ground pepper

1 cup (8 fl oz/250 ml) whole milk

2 eggs

1 teaspoon ground coriander

1/2 cup (1 oz/30 g) fine dried bread crumbs mixed with 1 teaspoon minced fresh flat-leaf (Italian) parsley

1/4 lb (125 g) fresh goat cheese, crumbled

Potato Nests with Sausage and Eggs

1 tablespoon vegetable oil

2 lb (1 kg) sweet or spicy Italian sausage, casings removed, shaped into 8 patties 1/2 inch (12 mm) thick

FOR THE POTATO NESTS:

1 1/2 lb (750 g) Yukon gold potatoes

Coarse salt and freshly ground pepper

About 1/3 cup (3 fl oz/80 ml) vegetable oil

FOR THE SPICY TOMATO SAUCE:

1/2 cup (4 fl oz/125 ml) tomato ketchup

1 1/2 tablespoons red pepper flakes

1 teaspoon Worcestershire sauce

1/2 teaspoon fresh lemon juice

8 eggs, poached (see page 291)

4–6 fresh flat-leaf (Italian) parsley sprigs

Preheat the oven to 200°F (95°C). In a large frying pan over high heat, warm the oil. Add the sausage patties and cook until browned on one side, about 3 minutes. Turn and brown on the second side, about 2 minutes longer. Reduce the heat to medium-low, cover partially, and continue cooking until the juices run clear when the patties are pierced with a fork, 10–12 minutes. Transfer to a plate, cover, and keep warm in the oven.

To make the potato nests, using the medium holes of a box grater shredder, grate the potatoes into a bowl. Add 2 1/2 teaspoons coarse salt and 1 teaspoon pepper and toss with a fork to mix. In a large, heavy frying pan over high heat, warm the oil until it shimmers. Meanwhile, squeeze the shredded potatoes dry between your hands and form them into 8 even-sized potato nests. Working quickly, slide each nest into the hot oil and fry until lightly browned on one side, about 10 minutes. Turn the potato nests and continue to fry until crisp and brown on the second side yet tender on the inside, about 10 minutes longer. Transfer to a baking sheet and keep warm in the low oven.

To make the tomato sauce, in a small bowl, whisk together the tomato ketchup, red pepper flakes, Worcestershire sauce, and lemon juice. Taste for seasoning and set aside.

To serve, place a potato nest on each serving plate. Top each with a sausage patty, a poached egg, and a spoonful of the tomato sauce. Garnish with the parsley sprigs. Serve at once, passing the remaining sauce at the table.

Serves 8

BREAKFAST & BRUNCH | 231

Asparagus and Potato Frittata

Italian frittatas are made by combining various ingredients—such as the spring vegetables and herbs shown here—with eggs and cooking the mixture on the stove top. Here, the process is simplified by finishing the frittata in the oven.

Place the spears in a steamer insert set in a saucepan over boiling water. Cover and steam until the asparagus is tender, about 2 minutes. Remove from the steamer and cut into 1-inch (2.5-cm) lengths. Set aside.

In a large sauté pan over medium heat, warm 3 tablespoons of the olive oil. Add the green onions and sauté until soft and translucent, about 4 minutes. Add the potatoes, tarragon, and salt and pepper to taste and sauté until the potatoes glisten, about 3 minutes, adding the remaining 1 tablespoon oil if needed to prevent sticking. Cover and cook until the potatoes are nearly tender, 6–8 minutes. Uncover, raise the heat to high, and cook, stirring constantly, until the potatoes are browned, 7–8 minutes. Stir in the chives and asparagus and remove from the heat.

Preheat the oven to 375°F (190°C). In a large cast-iron frying pan or ovenproof sauté pan over medium-high heat, melt the butter. Meanwhile, in a bowl, whisk the eggs until blended. Stir in a pinch of salt and the Parmesan cheese and season with pepper to taste. Pour the eggs into the hot pan. Stir gently in the center and, using a fork or spatula, carefully lift the edges and gently push the eggs to one side of the pan, tilting the pan slightly to allow the uncooked egg to flow underneath. Cook until thickened, 3–4 minutes. Spread the vegetables evenly over the eggs. Sprinkle the Swiss cheese on top. Place in the oven and bake until the eggs are set and the cheese melts, about 15 minutes. Remove from the oven and let stand for a few minutes, then cut into wedges and serve, garnished with the watercress sprigs and the chive blossoms, if desired.

Serves 8–10

3/4 lb (375 g) thin asparagus spears, tough ends removed

3–4 tablespoons olive oil

2 large green (spring) onions, chopped

6–8 small red potatoes, unpeeled, cut into slices 1/8 inch (3 mm) thick

1/2 teaspoon chopped fresh tarragon

Salt and freshly ground pepper

2 tablespoons snipped fresh chives, plus chive blossoms for garnish (optional)

3 tablespoons unsalted butter

11 eggs

1/3 cup (1 1/2 oz/45 g) grated Parmesan cheese

1/2 cup (2 oz/60 g) shredded Swiss cheese

1 bunch watercress, tough stems removed

Ginger Waffles with Raspberry Sauce and Ginger Cream

FOR THE RASPBERRY SAUCE:

3/4 lb (375 g) fresh or frozen unsweetened raspberries, thawed if frozen

1/2 cup (4 oz/125 g) granulated sugar

FOR THE GINGER CREAM:

1 cup (8 fl oz/250 ml) sour cream

1/4 cup (2 oz/60 g) granulated sugar

1 teaspoon peeled and minced fresh ginger

1 teaspoon grated lemon zest

FOR THE WAFFLES:

2 1/4 cups (9 oz/280 g) sifted all-purpose (plain) flour

1 tablespoon baking powder

3 eggs, separated

1/4 cup (2 oz/60 g) firmly packed golden brown sugar

1 3/4 cups (14 fl oz/430 ml) whole milk

6 tablespoons (3 oz/90 g) unsalted butter, melted

2 tablespoons peeled and minced fresh ginger

Pinch of salt

1/2 pint (4 oz/125 g) fresh raspberries (optional)

To make the sauce, in a food processor, process the berries and their juice until smooth, about 40 seconds. Strain through a sieve placed over a saucepan, pressing down with a spatula to extract as much liquid as possible. Discard the contents of the sieve. Add the sugar and place over medium heat. Stir until the sugar dissolves and the sauce is warm, 1–2 minutes, keep warm.

To make the ginger cream, in a small nonreactive bowl, whisk together the sour cream, sugar, ginger, and lemon zest. Cover and refrigerate. Preheat the oven to 200°F (95°C). Preheat a waffle iron. To make the waffles, in a bowl, stir together the flour and baking powder. In another bowl, combine the egg yolks and brown sugar. Using an electric mixer set on medium speed, beat the egg-sugar mixture until smooth and thick, 2–3 minutes. Add the milk, melted butter, and ginger and mix well with a spoon. Gradually stir in the flour mixture until no lumps remain.

In a clean bowl, and with clean beaters, beat together the egg whites and salt until stiff peaks form. Gently fold the beaten egg whites into the batter.

Ladle enough batter into the waffle iron for 1 waffle (consult the manufacturers directions). Close the iron and cook until the iron opens easily, or according to the manufacturer's directions. The waffle should be crisp and golden. Using a fork, carefully loosen the waffle from the iron. Transfer to a baking sheet and place in a warm oven. Repeat until all the batter is cooked.

To serve, drizzle the waffles with the warm raspberry sauce and top with a dollop of the cold ginger cream. Garnish, if desired, with fresh raspberries. Pass the remaining raspberry sauce and ginger cream at the table.

Serves 4

Asparagus and Garlic Omelet

This omelet is a perfect first course or part of a delightful brunch when asparagus is in season in the spring. For a more substantial dish, sauté ¼ pound (125 g) peeled and deveined shrimp (prawns) or lump crabmeat with the asparagus.

Snap off the tough ends from the asparagus where they break naturally and discard. Cut the spears on the diagnolinto 1-inch (2.5-cm) lengths. Bring a saucepan three-fourths full of water to a boil, add the asparagus, and parboil for 3 minutes. Drain, rinse with cold water, drain again, and pat dry.

In a medium sauté pan over low heat, warm 2 tablespoons of the olive oil. Add the shallots and sauté until softened, about 8 minutes. Add the chives, garlic, and asparagus and sauté, stirring, until the asparagus is tender, about 2 minutes. Remove from the heat.

In a bowl, whisk the eggs until blended. Add the asparagus mixture and season to taste with salt and pepper.

In an 8-inch (20-cm) omelet or sauté pan over high heat, warm the remaining 2 tablespoons olive oil. When very hot, pour in the egg mixture and immediately reduce the heat to medium. Cook, running a spatula around the edges of the pan a few times, until the underside is golden, 8–10 minutes. Invert a flat plate on top of the pan and, holding the plate and pan together firmly, carefully invert them. Lift off the pan, slide the omelet back into it, browned side up, and return to medium heat. Cook on the second side just until pale gold, about 4 minutes longer. Do not overcook, or the omelet will dry out.

Slide the omelet onto a serving plate, let cool slightly, and then cut into wedges and serve.

Serves 4

½ lb (250 g) thin asparagus spears

4 tablespoons (2 fl oz/60 ml) olive oil

2 shallots, finely chopped, or 6 green (spring) onions, including the tender green tops, finely chopped

8 fresh chives, snipped

2 cloves garlic, finely minced

5 large eggs

Salt and freshly ground pepper

Ham and Cheddar Cheese Gratin

Unsalted butter for greasing, plus 1¹/₂ tablespoons

¹/₄ cup (1¹/₂ oz/45 g) finely chopped yellow onion

1 celery rib, finely chopped

2 cups (14 oz/440 g) cubed baked ham

1 teaspoon chopped fresh tarragon

Pinch of freshly ground black pepper

FOR THE SAUCE:

¹/₄ cup (2 oz/60 g) unsalted butter

¹/₄ cup (1¹/₂ oz/45 g) all-purpose (plain) flour

4 cups (32 fl oz/1 l) whole milk, heated almost to a boil

2 teaspoons chopped fresh tarragon

¹/₄ teaspoon dry mustard

Pinch *each* of ground nutmeg and cayenne pepper

Freshly ground black pepper

³/₄ cup (3 oz/90 g) finely cubed Cheddar cheese, plus ¹/₄ cup (1 oz/30 g), shredded

6 hard-boiled eggs, peeled

1–2 tablespoons heavy (double) cream

Preheat the oven to 400°F (200°C). Butter a 1¹/₂-qt (1¹/₂-l) gratin dish or other shallow round or oval baking dish.

In a small sauté pan over medium heat, melt the 1¹/₂ tablespoons butter. When the foam subsides, add the onion and celery and sauté until soft and translucent, about 3 minutes. Add the ham and sauté until heated through, about 2 minutes. Mix in the tarragon and season to taste with pepper. Scatter the ham mixture over the bottom of the prepared dish. Set aside.

To make the sauce, in a heavy saucepan over medium-high heat, melt the butter. Add the flour and cook, stirring constantly, for 2 minutes without letting the flour brown, adjusting the heat as needed. Remove from the heat. Add the hot milk all at once and whisk vigorously to prevent lumps from forming. Return the pan to the heat and cook, stirring constantly, until thickened, about 2 minutes. Add the tarragon, dry mustard, nutmeg, cayenne, and black peppers to taste. Stir in the cubed Cheddar cheese. Taste and adjust the seasonings.

Cut the hard-boiled eggs in half lengthwise; set 6 halves aside. Coarsely chop the remaining egg halves and stir them into the warm sauce. Pour all but about ¹/₄ cup (2 fl oz/60 ml) of the sauce over the ham mixture. Then, nest the reserved egg halves, yolk sides up, in the sauce, spacing them evenly so they indicate the center of a serving. Whisk the cream into the reserved sauce to thin it to a spreadable consistency, then pour over the eggs. Scatter the shredded Cheddar cheese over the top.

Bake until the sauce is bubbling and the surface is golden brown, 10–12 minutes. Serve directly from the dish.

Serves 6

Pecan Waffles with Maple-Pear Sauce

To make the sauce, place the pear slices in a bowl and toss with the lemon juice. In a large, nonreactive saucepan over medium heat, melt the butter. Add the pears and sauté gently just to coat with butter, 1–2 minutes. Add $^1/_4$ cup (2 fl oz/60 ml) water, the lemon zest, and maple syrup, reduce the heat to low, and simmer just until the pears are tender but still hold their shape, about 6 minutes. Using a slotted spoon, transfer the pears to a bowl. Raise the heat to high and reduce the cooking liquid to about 1 cup (8 fl oz/250 ml), about 10 minutes. Pour $^1/_2$ cup (4 fl oz/125 ml) of the reduced liquid over the pears; reserve the remaining syrup separately. Keep warm or bring to room temperature.

Put the pecans in a small, dry frying pan over medium-low heat and toast, stirring constantly, until fragrant, 2–3 minutes. Remove the nuts from the frying pan and set aside. Preheat the oven to 200°F (95°C). Preheat a waffle iron.

In a bowl, sift together the flour, sugar, baking powder, and salt. In a small bowl, whisk together the milk, egg yolks, melted butter, and vanilla. In a third bowl, using an electric mixer and clean beaters, beat together the egg whites and cream of tartar until stiff peaks form. Stir the milk mixture into the dry ingredients, beating until smooth, then stir in the pecans. Finally, using a rubber spatula, old the egg whites into the batter, leaving tiny clouds of whites visible. The batter will look sandy.

Ladle enough batter into the waffle iron for 1 waffle (consult the manufacturer's directions). Close the iron and cook until the iron opens easily, or according to the manufacturer's directions. The waffle should be crisp and golden. Using a fork, carefully loosen the waffle from the iron. Transfer to a bakin gsheet and place in the warm oven. Repeat until all the batter is cooked.

To serve, top the waffles with the pear sauce. Pass the reserved syrup at the table.

Makes 6–8 waffles

FOR THE MAPLE PEAR SAUCE:

4 firm yet ripe Anjou or Bartlett (Williams) pears, peeled, halved, cored, and cut into slices 1/4 inch (6 mm) thick

Juice of 1 lemon

1/4 cup (2 oz/60 g) unsalted butter

Grated zest of 1/2 lemon

1 cup (11 oz/345 g) pure maple syrup, preferably Grade B

1/2 cup (2 oz/60 g) finely chopped pecans

1³/4 cups (9 oz/280 g) all-purpose (plain) flour

1 tablespoon sugar

2 teaspoons baking powder

1/4 teaspoon salt

1³/4 cups (14 fl oz/430 ml) whole milk

3 eggs, separated

6 tablespoons (3 oz/90 g) butter, melted and cooled

1/2 teaspoon vanilla extract (essence)

Pinch of cream of tartar

Red, White, and Blueberry Fruit Bowl

Put the blueberries in a glass serving bowl or divide them evenly among 4 individual glass bowls.

Using a small, sharp knife, remove the green stems and hulls from the strawberries. Put the strawberries in the bowl(s) with the blueberries.

Peel the bananas and cut them into $^1/_2$-inch-thick rounds. Add the bananas rounds to the bowl(s), arranging them on top of the berries. Mix the fruit gently with a spoon.

Spoon the yogurt on top of the fruit. Sprinkle the brown sugar and then the granola over the yogurt. Serve immediately.

Serves 4

1 cup (4 oz/125 g) blueberries

20 large strawberries

2 large bananas

2 cups (16 oz/500 g) plain yogurt

2 tablespoons firmly packed dark brown sugar

1 cup (6 oz/185 g) granola

Raspberry Corn Muffins

Tangy fresh raspberries and sweet raspberry preserves fill the center of these light corn muffins, adding a surprise to every mouthful. They are a wonderful treat and a great addition to an afternoon tea tray.

Preheat the oven to 450°F (230°C). Generously grease a standard 12-cup muffin-pan with the shortening, or line the cups with foil or paper liners.

In a small saucepan over low heat, melt the butter. Remove from the heat and let cool. In a small bowl, whisk the eggs until frothy, then whisk in the buttermilk. Set both aside.

In a sieve placed over a bowl, combine the cornmeal, flour, sugar, baking powder, salt, and baking soda. Shake the sieve to pass the mixture through. Add the orange zest and stir to mix. Make a well in the center. Whisk the melted butter into the egg mixture, then pour the egg mixture into the well. Using a fork, mix just until the dry ingredients are moistened. The batter will look lumpy.

Spoon the batter into the prepared muffin cups, filling each one half full. Sprinkle a few raspberries into each cup, and then top with a dab of the raspberry preserves, dividing evenly. Spoon the remaining batter over the top to cover the fruit, filling each cup about two-thirds full.

Bake the muffins until light brown on top, firm to the touch, and the edges have pulled away from the sides of the cups, 15–20 minutes. Remove from the oven, invert onto a wire rack, and serve immediately.

Makes 12 muffins

Vegetable shortening (vegetable lard) (optional)

1/4 cup (2 oz/60 g) unsalted butter

2 eggs, beaten

1 1/2 cups (12 fl oz/375 ml) buttermilk

1 1/2 cups (7 1/2 oz/235 g) stone-ground yellow cornmeal

1/2 cup (2 1/2 oz/75 g) all-purpose (plain) flour

2 tablespoons sugar

2 teaspoons baking powder

1 teaspoon salt

1/2 teaspoon baking soda (bicarbonate of soda)

Grated zest of 1 orange

1 cup (4 oz/125 g) raspberries

2 tablespoons raspberry preserves

Smoked Salmon Scrambled Eggs

Keeping the heat low and using a good amount of butter creates creamy, soft, buttery scrambled eggs. Serve with toasted bagels for brunch, or add asparagus and open a bottle of Champagne for a late-night supper.

4 tablespoons (2 oz/60 g) unsalted butter

4 green (spring) onions, white part and about 2 inches (5 cm) of the green tops, chopped

8 eggs

1/4–1/2 teaspoon freshly ground pepper

3 oz (90 g) smoked salmon, chopped

3 oz (90 g) cream cheese, cut into 1/4-inch (6-mm) cubes, at room temperature

Fresh tarragon sprigs for garnish (optional)

In a large, heavy nonstick sauté pan over low heat, melt the butter. Set aside 2 tablespoons of the green onions to use for garnish and add the remaining green onions to the pan. Sauté until soft and translucent, about 3 minutes.

Meanwhile, in a bowl, using a fork, beat the eggs with pepper to taste until blended. Pour the eggs into the sauté pan over low heat and, using a wooden spoon, continuously stir, reaching the bottom and edges of the pan, until the eggs begin to thicken and break into curds, about 5 minutes. Keep stirring until the eggs are almost firm, about 4 minutes.

Remove the pan from the heat and fold the salmon and cream cheese into the eggs. Return the pan to low heat for about 30 seconds to melt the cheese. Transfer to warmed plates or a warmed platter, sprinkle with the reserved green onions, and garnish with tarragon sprigs, if you like. Serve at once.

Serves 4

Steak and Eggs

To make the caramelized onions, preheat the oven to 375°F (190°C). In a small baking dish, place the garlic and stock. Drizzle 2 tablespoons of the olive oil over the top. Cover and bake until the garlic is soft, about 35 minutes. Let cool, covered, for 10 minutes, then uncover, let cool, peel, and slice the garlic; set aside.

Meanwhile, brush 2 large rimmed baking sheets with 2 tablespoons each of the olive oil. Divide the onions evenly between the prepared baking sheets and season with salt and pepper. Sprinkle 1 1/2 tablespoons of the brown sugar evenly over the onions, then drizzle about 2 tablespoons oil over each pan. Bake, stirring every 15 minutes, until golden brown, about 45 minutes. Remove from the oven and stir in the cooled garlic. In a small bowl, stir together the vinegar, the remaining 2 1/2 tablespoons brown sugar, and cayenne pepper to taste, then drizzle it evenly over the onions. Return the onion mixture to the oven and bake until evenly browned and caramelized, about 20 minutes longer. Transfer to a bowl. Taste and adjust the seasonings; keep warm.

While the onions are cooking, score the edges of the steaks every inch (2.5 cm) or so. Rub 1 teaspoon coarse pepper on both sides and let stand for 5–10 minutes. Place a large, well-seasoned cast-iron or nonstick frying pan over high heat and sprinkle with a pinch of coarse salt. Add the steaks and sear, turning once, until browned on both sides, about 2 minutes per side for rare, or until done to your liking.

Meanwhile, in a nonstick sauté pan over medium heat, melt the butter. Break the eggs into the pan, immediately reduce the heat to low, cover, and cook until the whites are set and the yolks are glazed but still liquid, 3–5 minutes, or until done as desired. Season to taste with salt and pepper.

Transfer the steaks to warmed individual plates and place the eggs alongside. Spoon a generous serving of the caramelized onions over the the steaks and serve.

Serves 6

FOR THE CARAMELIZED ONIONS:

3 heads garlic, unpeeled and cloves separated

1/2 cup (4 fl oz/125 ml) Chicken Stock (page 288) or broth

Olive oil

8 large red onions, thinly sliced

Salt and freshly ground black pepper

4 tablespoons (2 oz/60 g) firmly packed dark brown sugar

2 tablespoons balsamic vinegar

Cayenne pepper

6 New York strip steaks, each about 1/2 lb (250 g) and 1 inch (2.5 cm) thick, trimmed of excess fat

Coarsely ground black pepper

Coarse salt

2 1/2 tablespoons unsalted butter

6 eggs

Omelet with Spinach and Blue Cheese

A great way to experiment with traditional omelets is to add different fillings. Choose a mild blue cheese or goat cheese for this recipe. A strong blue such as Roquefort, Maytag, or Gorgonzola would overwhelm the delicate eggs.

1 lb (500 g) spinach leaves, tough stems removed

1 tablespoon olive oil

3 small cloves garlic, minced

Salt and freshly ground pepper

1 dozen eggs

2 tablespoons unsalted butter

4 oz (125 g) mild blue cheese, such as Cambozola, or fresh goat cheese, crumbled, at room temperature

Rinse and drain the spinach, then put into an 8- to 10-inch (20- to 25-cm) nonstick frying pan or omelet pan with just the rinsing water clinging to the leaves. Cover and cook over medium heat until the spinach wilts, about 3 minutes. Transfer to a sieve and press on the spinach with the back of a wooden spoon to squeeze out the excess moisture. Chop the spinach coarsely.

Preheat the oven to 200°F (95°C). Rinse and dry the frying pan. Return it to medium heat and add the olive oil. When the oil is hot, add the garlic and sauté for 1 minute to release its fragrance. Add the spinach, season lightly with salt and pepper, and cook until hot throughout. Transfer to a plate. In a bowl, season 3 of the eggs with salt and pepper and whisk to blend. Return the frying pan to medium-high heat and add 1 teaspoon of the butter. When the butter melts, add the eggs. Using a heatproof rubber spatula, stir the eggs briskly until they begin to set. Allow them to set on the bottom without stirring further, then lift the edges of the omelet with the fork or spatula to allow the uncooked egg to flow underneath.

When the surface is cooked but still moist, put one-fourth each of the spinach and cheese on the two-thirds of the omelet farthest from the pan handle. Using the fork or spatula, fold the closest third of the omelet over onto the middle third. With a warmed dinner plate in one hand and the pan in the other, slide the outer third of the omelet onto the plate, then tilt the pan to flip the rest of the omelet over. Repeat process for additional 3 omelets. Transfer each omelet, as ready to a baking sheet and place in the preheated oven while you work.

Serves 4

Lemon Pancakes with Blueberry Sauce

In a saucepan over low heat, stir together 1 cup (8 fl oz/250 ml) water, 5 tablespoons (3 fl oz/80 ml) of the lemon juice, and cornstarch until the cornstarch dissolves, about 2 minutes. Add 2¹/₂ cups (10 oz/315 g) of the blueberries and raise the heat to medium. Cook, stirring, until the sauce thickens and coats a spoon, about 5 minutes. Let cool slightly, then transfer to a food processor or blender. Purée until smooth, then pass through a sieve placed over the saucepan, pressing down with a spatula to extract as much liquid as possible. Add the 5 tablespoons (2¹/₂ oz/75 g) granulated sugar and stir in the remaining 1¹/₂ cups (6 oz/185 g) blueberries. Place over medium heat and cook, stirring, until the berries soften slightly, 1–2 minutes. Stir in the cinnamon. Taste and add more sugar, if needed. Keep warm.

Preheat the oven to 200°F (95°C). In a large bowl, whisk together the flour, ¹/₂ cup (4 oz/125 g) granulated sugar, baking powder, baking soda, and salt. In another bowl, whisk together the milk, sour cream, eggs, the melted butter, the remaining 6 tablespoons (3 fl oz/90 ml) lemon juice, and 3 teaspoons of the zest. Pour the milk mixture over the flour mixture and stir just until combined.

Place a large, heavy frying pan over medium heat. Brush the pan lightly with some of the oil. Using a ¹/₄-cup (2-fl oz/60-ml) measure, ladle the batter into the pan, keeping the pancakes about 1/2 inch apart. Cook until small bubbles appear on the surfaces and the bottoms are lightly browned, 2–3 minutes. Using a spatula, flip the pancakes and cook until the second sides are golden, 1–2 minutes longer. Transfer to a baking sheet and place in the warm oven. Repeat with the remaining batter adding more oil as needed. You should have 24 pancakes.

Serve the pancakes on warmed individual plates, with the warm sauce and the remaining 1¹/₂ teaspoons lemon zest. Dust with confectioners' sugar. Pass the remaining sauce at the table.

Serves 6

11 tablespoons (5¹/₂ fl oz/ 165 ml) fresh lemon juice

2 tablespoons cornstarch (cornflour)

4 cups (1 lb/500 g) fresh blueberries, thawed and well drained if frozen

5 tablespoons (2¹/₂ oz/75 g) granulated sugar, or as needed, plus ¹/₂ cup (4 oz/125 g)

¹/₈ teaspoon ground cinnamon

2 cups (10 oz/315 g) all-purpose (plain) flour

2 teaspoons baking powder

1 teaspoon baking soda (bicarbonate of soda)

¹/₂ teaspoon salt

1¹/₂ cups (12 fl oz/375 ml) whole milk

1 cup (8 fl oz/250 ml) sour cream

2 eggs

Melted butter

4¹/₂ teaspoons grated lemon zest

Vegetable oil

Confectioners' (icing) sugar for dusting

Spinach and Feta Quiche

FOR THE EGG PASTRY:

3 cups (15 oz/470 g)
all-purpose (plain) flour

1/2 teaspoon salt

1 cup (8 oz/250 g) chilled
unsalted butter

1 egg

3/4 cup (3 oz/90 g) shredded
Swiss cheese

2 packages (10 oz/315 g each)
thawed frozen chopped spinach

1 tablespoon unsalted butter

2 tablespoons olive oil

1/4 cup (1 1/2 oz/45 g) finely
chopped yellow onion

10 green (spring) onions, chopped

1 clove garlic, minced

2/3 cup (1 oz/30 g) chopped
fresh dill

1 teaspoon freshly ground
pepper

3 eggs

1 cup (8 fl oz/250 ml)
half-and-half (half cream)

1/2 cup (4 fl oz/125 ml) heavy
(double) cream

1/4 lb (125 g) feta cheese

1/4 cup (1 1/2 oz/45 g) pitted
Kalamata olives, chopped

To make the pastry, in a bowl, stir together the flour and salt. Cut the butter into small pieces and add to the bowl. Using a pastry blender, cut it in until the mixture resembles coarse meal. In a small bowl, using a fork, beat the egg with 2 tablespoons ice water. Make a well in the flour mixture and pour in the egg mixture and 2 more tablespoons ice water. Using the fork, mix lightly, adding more ice water as needed until the mixture holds together. Pat the pastry into a ball, wrap in plastic wrap, and refrigerate for 1 hour.

On a floured work surface, roll out the pastry into a round 13 inches (33 cm) in diameter. Transfer to an 11-inch (28-cm) fluted tart pan with a removable bottom, and fit the dough in the pan. Cut off any excess dough and prick the bottom in several places with a fork. Press a piece of aluminum foil, shiny side down, onto the crust and freeze for about 30 minutes. Preheat the oven to 425°F (220°C). Bake the foil-lined pastry shell for 8 minutes. Remove the foil and continue baking until the crust looks dull, about 4 minutes longer. Remove from the oven, sprinkle with the Swiss cheese, and reduce the oven temperature to 375°F (190°C).

Drain the spinach and squeeze dry. In a large sauté pan over medium heat, melt the butter with the oil. Add the yellow and green onions and garlic and sauté until soft, about 4 minutes. Add the spinach and sauté, stirring, until completely wilted, about 3 minutes. Add the dill and pepper and continue sautéing, about 2 minutes longer. Taste and adjust the seasonings. Let cool for 5–6 minutes. In bowl, whisk the eggs until blended, then whisk in the half-and-half and cream. Crumble the feta cheese into the spinach and stir in the cream mixture. Pour into the prebaked shell. Bake until the filling is puffed and light brown and a knife inserted into the center comes out clean, 35–40 minutes. Remove from the oven and let stand for 5–10 minutes. Garnish with the olives, cut into wedges and serve.

Serves 6

Desserts

Lemon-Almond Butter Cake

1³/₄ cups (5¹/₂ oz/170 g) sifted cake (soft-wheat) flour

2 teaspoons baking powder

¹/₂ teaspoon salt

2 lemons

¹/₂ cup (4 oz/125 g) unsalted butter, at room temperature

1 cup (8 oz/250 g) sugar

2 eggs, beaten

¹/₂ cup (4 fl oz/125 ml) whole milk

1¹/₂ cups Lemon Curd (page 291)

¹/₂ cup (2 oz/60 g) sliced (flaked) almonds, toasted

Position a rack in the middle of the oven and preheat to 350°F (150°C).

Butter an 8-inch (20-cm) round cake pan with 2-inch (5-cm) sides. Cut out a piece of waxed paper to fit the bottom of the pan and slip into place. Butter the paper, then dust the paper and the pan sides with flour. Tap out any excess.

In a large bowl, sift together the flower, baking powder, and salt. Set aside. Using the small holes on a box grater-shredder, grate the zest from the lemons. Be sure to include all the zest clinging to the grater. Set aside.

In a large bowl, combine the butter and sugar. Using an electric mixer set on medium speed, beat until light and creamy, about 5 minutes, scraping down the sides of the bowl 3 or 4 times. Add the beaten eggs to the butter mixture, a little at a time, beating thoroughly after each addition, then continue beating until doubled in volume, 4–5 minutes, again scraping down the sides of the bowl 3 or 4 times. Beat in the lemon zest. Using a rubber spatula, carefully fold in the flour mixture, one-third at a time, alternating with the milk. Spoon into the prepared pan, building up the sides higher than the center.

Bake until the top is golden, 35–40 minutes. Insert a toothpick into the center; it should come out clean. Remove the cake from the oven and it rest for a couple of minutes. Using a knife, loosen the sides of the cake from the pan and turn out, bottom side up, onto a wire rack. Peel off the paper and let cool completely.

Transfer the cooled cake, bottom side up, to a flat plate. Using a long, sharp knife, cut the cake in half horizontally, forming 2 layers. Spread a thin layer of the Lemon Curd on the bottom layer. Replace the top layer and spread the remaining curd over the top and sides of the cake. Arrange the toasted almonds over the top and sides. Cut into wedges and serve.

Serves 10

Poached Pears and Blueberries

In a large saucepan, combine 4 cups (32 fl oz/1 l) water, the sugar, and the juice of 1 of the lemons. Place over medium-high heat and bring to a boil, stirring to dissolve the sugar. Remove the resulting syrup from the heat and set aside.

Working from the bottom of each pear, carefully remove the core, cutting no farther than three-fourths of the way toward the stem send. Do not remove the stem. Peel the pears and, if necessary, cut a thin slice off the bottom of each to make them stand upright. Place the pears in the syrup, return the pan to the heat, and quickly bring back to a boil. Lower the heat and simmer, turning occasionally, until the pears are tender when pierced with the tip of a sharp knife, 20–25 minutes. Using a slotted spoon, transfer the pears to a dish to cool. Reserve $^1/_2$ cup (4 fl oz/ 125 ml) of the syrup; refrigerate the remaining syrup for another use.

In a saucepan, combine the blueberries and the $^1/_2$ cup (fl oz/125 ml) reserved poaching syrup. Place over medium heat and bring just to a simmer. Reduce the heat slightly and simmer uncovered until the berries are tender, 10–15 minutes. Set aside to cool.

When ready to serve, transfer the pears, stem ends up, to individual dessert plates and spoon the blueberries around them. Dribble some of the blueberries over the pears, as well, if you like. Using the small holes of a box grater-shredder, and holding the remaining lemon over each plate, grate the zest from the lemons evenly over the top. Be sure to include all the zest clinging to the grater. Serve with the whipped cream spooned over each pear.

Serves 4

3 cups (24 oz/750 g) sugar

2 lemons

4 firm but ripe pears such as Comice, Bosc, or Bartlett (Williams'), preferably with their stems attached

2 cups (8 oz/250 g) blueberries

Lightly sweetened whipped cream for serving

Pink Grapefruit Granita

6 or 7 pink grapefruits, preferably Texas Ruby

1 cup (8 fl oz/250 g) sugar

2 fresh mint sprigs, or as needed, plus extra sprigs for garnish

Orange zest strips for garnish (optional)

Be sure your freezer is set at its coldest setting an hour before you being to make the granita. Squeeze the juice from the grapefruits and strain the juice through a fine-mesh sieve into a bowl. You will need $3-3^{1}/_2$ cups (24–28 fl oz/750–875 ml). Cover and refrigerate until well chilled.

In a saucepan over medium heat, combine $^{1}/_2$ cup (4 fl oz/125 ml) water and the sugar. Bring to a boil, stirring to dissolve the sugar. Using a brush moistened with water, brush down the pan sides to remove and sugar crystals. Add the 2 mint sprigs and boil for 1 minute. Set aside until cool enough to taste, 5–10 minutes, then taste for flavor. If the syrup has a good mint flavor remove and discard the mint; if not, add more mint and repeat the boiling and cooling process. Set aside to cool completely.

When the syrup has cooled, stir it into the chilled grapefruit juice until completely blended. Pour this mixture into a shallow stainless steel bowl or another stainless steel container. (Ice-cube trays will work if you have nothing else on hand.) Place in the freezer.

After about 20 minutes, check to see if any ice crystals have formed. If they have, stir to break them up with a fork. Continue to check every 15–20 minutes and stir as necessary to prevent the crystals from forming a sold mass. Frequent stirring is important to producing a uniformly textured granita. Be sure to scrape any frozen crystals from the sides and bottom of the container and break them up each time. The granita should freeze in $1^{1}/_2$–2 hours; it may take up to 3 hours.

To serve, place 4–6 footed glass goblets in the refrigerator 10–15 minutes before serving. Spoon the granita into the chilled goblets. Garnish with mint sprigs and orange zest strips, if desired. Serve at once.

Serves 4–6

Lime-Pecan Butter Cookies

Light and crunchy, these butter cookies are flavored with just a hint of lime. For the best results, weigh your ingredients carefully, and be careful not to make the cookies too big: Form balls of dough no more that 1 inch (2.5 cm) in diameter.

Position a rack in the middle of the oven and preheat to 350°F (180°C). Butter 2 baking sheets.

In a bowl, sift together the flour, cornstarch, and salt. Set aside. In a food processor fitted with the metal blade or in a blender in two batches, combine ¹/₄ cup (2 oz/60 g) of the sugar and the pecans. Pulse until finely chopped. Set aside.

Using the small holes on a box grater-shredder, and holding the grater above a saucer, grate the zest from the lime. Be sure to include all the zest clinging to the grater. You should have about ¹/₂ teaspoon. Cut the lime in half and squeeze the juice into a small bowl. Remove any seeds. Set the zest and the juice aside.

In a bowl, combine the remaining ¹/₂ cup (4 oz/125 g) sugar and the butter. Using an electric mixer set on medium speed, beat until light, about 5 minutes. Add the egg white, lime zest, and 2 teaspoons of the lime juice and continue beating until fluffy, another 8–10 minutes, scraping down the sides of the bowl as needed. Reduce the speed to low and carefully beat in the flour mixture, a little at a time. Add the pecan mixture and beat until well blended. Using a small spoon, scoop up spoonfuls of the dough and, using your hands, form them into balls about 1 inch (2.5 cm) in diameter. Place on the prepared baking sheets about 1 inch (2.5 cm) apart. Using a thumb, press down on each ball to flatten it to about ³/₈ inch (9 mm) thick. Bake until the cookies just begin to color at the edges, 18–20 minutes. Transfer the baking sheets to wire racks to cool for 3–4 minutes, then transfer the cookies to the racks to cool completely before serving. Store in airtight containers.

Makes 60–65 cookies

2 cups (10 oz/315 g) all-purpose (plain) flour

¹/₄ cup (1 oz/30 g) cornstarch (cornflour)

¹/₄ teaspoon salt

³/₄ cup (6 oz/185 g) sugar

1 cup pecans, halved

1 lime

³/₄ cup (6 oz/185 g) unsalted butter, cut into cubes

1 egg white

Oranges with Mint and Toasted Almonds

6 navel oranges

1 cup (8 oz/250 g) sugar

3 or 4 large mint sprigs, plus leaves for garnish

3/4 cup (3 oz/90 g) sliced (flaked) almonds, toasted

Using a small paring knife, peel the zest (not the white pith) from 2 of the oranges, removing it in long pieces. Slice the zest into strips $1/8$ inch (3 mm) wide and about 2 inches (5 cm) long. Fill a saucepan half full of water and bring it to a boil over medium heat. Add the orange zest strips, reduce the heat to medium-low, and simmer, uncovered, for 15 minutes. Drain and set aside.

In a saucepan over medium-high heat, combine 1 cup (8 fl oz/250 ml) water and the sugar. Bring to a boil, stirring to dissolve the sugar. Using a brush moistened with water, brush down the pan sides to remove any sugar crystals. Reduce the heat to low, add the 3 or 4 mint sprigs, and simmer until the syrup is nicely mint-flavored, 5–6 minutes. Remove the mint sprigs and discard.

Add the reserved orange zest strips and simmer over medium-low heat until the syrup has thickened and the zest is translucent, 12–15 minutes. Brush down the pan sides again if you see any sugar crystals forming. Set aside to cool.

Cut off a thick slice from the top and bottom of the 2 partially peeled oranges, exposing the fruit beneath the peel. Then do the same to the 4 remaining oranges. Working with 1 orange at a time, place it upright on a cutting board and, holding the orange firmly, and following the contour of the fruit, slice off the peel in strips, cutting off the pith and membrane with it to reveal the fruit beneath. Cut the orange in half crosswise and place in a bowl. When all of the oranges have been peeled and cut, cover and refrigerate until chilled.

To serve, place 2 or 3 orange halves on dessert plates. Spoon the syrup and orange strips over the orange halves and sprinkle generously with the toasted almonds. Garnish with the fresh mint leaves and serve immediately.

Serves 4–6

Roast Bananas with Cinnamon Ice Cream and Chocolate Sauce

In this dessert, the heavy cream and the banana juices meld into a thick sauce while roasting. If you cannot find cinnamon-flavored ice cream, substitute vanilla ice cream sprinkled with ground cinnamon.

Preheat the oven to 375°F (190°C).

Arrange the bananas in a 9-inch (23-cm) pie dish or baking dish. Lightly dust them with the cinnamon, nutmeg, and sugar to taste. Drizzle in enough cream to cover the bottom of the dish.

Roast until the bananas are soft when pierced with a knife but still hold their shape and the reduced cream forms a bubbly sauce, about 30 minutes.

Meanwhile, make the chocolate sauce: In a large heatproof bowl set over (but not touching) simmering water in a saucepan, melt the chocolate. Pour in the cream in a steady stream, whisking constantly until well incorporated. The chocolate may "seize," that is, become lumpy for a moment or two. Just continue to whisk until the sauce becomes smooth. Stir in the vanilla; taste and adjust the flavorings. Keep hot. You should have about 2½ cups (20 fl oz/625 ml).

When the bananas are ready, arrange them on individual plates, and drizzle their bubbly sauce over them. Serve with a scoop of cinnamon ice cream drizzled with 1 tablespoon of the hot chocolate sauce. Pass the remaining hot chocolate sauce at the table.

Serves 6

6 large, firm yet ripe bananas, peeled and left whole

¼ teaspoon ground cinnamon

¼ teaspoon freshly grated nutmeg

1–2 tablespoons sugar

About 2 tablespoons heavy (double) cream

FOR THE CHOCOLATE SAUCE:

12 oz (375 g) semisweet (plain) chocolate, cut into chunks

1½–1⅔ cups (12–13 fl oz/ 375–410 ml) heavy (double) cream

1 tablespoon vanilla extract (essence), or to taste

1½ qt (1.5 l) cinnamon ice cream (see note)

Golden Apple Cobbler

If you find pastry-making difficult, or for a short cut to turning out a dessert with a classic flaky crust, try this deep-dish cobbler—every bit the equal of a traditional apple pie. Serve with lightly sweetened whipped cream.

3 lb (1.5 kg) Golden Delicious apples, peeled, cored, and thinly sliced

1/2 cup (4 oz/125 g) sugar

1 1/2 tablespoons all-purpose (plain) flour

1/4 cup (2 oz/60 g) unsalted butter

2 tablespoons fresh lemon juice

1 teaspoon vanilla extract (essence)

FOR THE CRUST:

2 cups (10 oz/315 g) all-purpose (plain) flour, plus flour for dusting

1/4 cups (2 oz/60 g) sugar

2 teaspoons baking powder

1/4 teaspoon salt

2 tablespoons cold unsalted butter, cut into small cubes

1/3 cup (3/4 oz/20 g) coarsely chopped crystallized ginger

1 orange

1 cup (8 fl oz/250 ml) heavy (double) cream, plus cream for brushing

Position a rack in the middle of the oven and preheat to 425°F (220° C). Butter a 1 1/2-q (1.5-l) pie dish 10 inches (25 cm) in diameter and 2 inches (5 cm) deep.

In a bowl, stir together the sugar and the flour. In a large sauté pan over medium heat, melt the butter. Stir in the apples, lemon juice, and sugar mixture. Cover and cook, stirring occasionally, until tender, 15–20 minutes. Stir in the vanilla. Let cool for 15–20 minutes, then transfer to the prepared dish.

To make the crust, whisk together the flour, sugar, baking powder, and salt in a bowl. Add the butter and, using a pastry blender, 2 knives, or your fingertips, cut in the butter until the mixture resembles coarse crumbs. Stir in the ginger.

Using the small holes of a box grater-shredder, grate the zest from the orange into a bowl. Be sure to include all the zest clinging to the grater. Stir in the 1 cup (8 fl oz/250 ml) cream. Then, using a fork, stir in the cream-zest mixture into the flour mixture, just until it holds together. Gather the dough into a ball. On a floured work surface and with floured hands, knead briefly until soft, then roll out the dough so it's a little larger than the pie dish. Transfer the dough round to the dish holding the apples; trim off the excess. Cut a small hole in the center for the steam to escape. Cut any scraps into fanciful shapes. Brush the top with cream where you wish to decorate, then press the shapes into place. Lightly brush the crust and decorations with cream.

Bake for 10 minutes. Reduce the oven heat to 375°F (190°C) and bake until golden, 20–25 minutes longer. Let cool on a wire rack. Cut into wedges and serve warm.

Serves 10

Ginger Cookies

Tiny chunks of crystallized ginger dot these sweet cookies, which can be made a day in advance of serving. Be sure not to overbake them or they will become hard and brittle. You can store the cookies in an airtight container up to 1 week.

In a bowl, using an electric mixer, beat together the butter and sugar until light and fluffy, about 4 minutes. Beat in the egg. In another bowl, whisk together the flour, baking soda, and salt. Beat the flour mixture into the butter mixture. Using a spoon or spatula, stir in the ginger and vanilla. Divide the dough in half.

On a lightly floured work surface, roll each piece of dough into a log about 1 1/2 inches (4 cm) in diameter. Wrap the logs separately in plastic wrap, place on a baking sheet, and refrigerate overnight.

Preheat the oven to 325°F (165°C). Lightly grease 2 baking sheets or line the bottoms with parchment (baking) paper.

Unwrap the logs and, using a sharp knife, cut each log into slices 1/2 inch (12 mm) thick. Carefully place on the prepared baking sheets, spacing them about 1 inch (2.5 cm) apart.

Bake, one sheet at a time, until the cookies are lightly browned around the edges, 8–10 minutes. Remove from the oven and transfer the cookies to wire racks. Let cool completely and serve. Store in airtight containers.

Makes about 30 cookies

1/2 cup (4 oz/125 g) unsalted butter, at room temperature

1 cup (7 oz/220 g) firmly packed golden brown sugar, or 1 cup (8 oz/250 g) granulated sugar

1 egg

1 3/4 cups (9 oz/280 g) all-purpose (plain) flour

1/2 teaspoon baking soda (bicarbonate of soda)

1/4 teaspoon salt

1/2 cup (1 1/2 oz/45 g) finely chopped crystallized ginger

1/2 teaspoon vanilla extract (essence)

Ricotta, Marmalade, and Chocolate Spread

FOR THE CANDIED
ORANGE PEEL:

2 oranges, zest removed in
large strips

1 tablespoon sea salt

1 cup (8 oz/250 g) sugar, plus
more for coating

1/2 cup water (4 fl oz/125 ml)
water

3 tablespoons light corn syrup

1 cup (8 oz/250 g) ricotta
cheese, preferably whole milk

1/4 cup (2 oz/60 g) mascarpone
cheese or cream cheese, at
room temperature

1/2 cup (5 oz/155 g) orange
marmalade

3 oz (90 g) bittersweet or
semisweet (plain) chocolate,
finely chopped

To make the candied orange peel, place 4 large zest pieces and the salt and add water just to cover. Stir to dissolve salt and let stand for about 5 hours. Drain and place the peel in a small saucepan, with water to cover. Bring to a boil over medium-high heat. Reduce heat to medium-low, and simmer, uncovered, for 15 minutes. Drain and repeat the process. Set aside.

Once cool enough to handle, cut the peel into strips $^1/4$ inch (6 mm) wide. In a small saucepan over medium heat, combine the sugar, water, and corn syrup. Heat, stirring until the mixture comes to a boil and the sugar is dissolved. Add the orange strips, reduce heat to low, and cook slowly until the strips are translucent, about 45–60 minutes. Do not allow to caramelize.

Transfer the orange strips to a wire rack to drain, spreading them out so the strips do not touch. While the strips are still warm, sprinkle with sugar until thoroughly coated. Place on a piece of waxed paper to cool completely.

Meanwhile, make the spread: In a food processor, process the ricotta cheese until smooth. Add the mascarpone or cream cheese and process until blended. Add the marmalade and process until incorporated but some small chunks remain. Add the chocolate and pulse until just blended (do not purée).

Transfer the mixture to a small bowl. Cover and refrigerate until well chilled, about 2 hours. Garnish with a few pieces of Candied Orange Peel; reserve the rest for another use.

Serves 6

Coconut-Banana Pancake Rolls

To make the pancakes, in a large bowl, combine the flour, granulated sugar, coconut, baking powder, and salt. Add the mashed banana, egg, and 1 3/4 cups (14 fl oz/430 ml) of the coconut milk and stir to combine. The batter should have a thin consistency. If it is too thick, add some or all of the remaining 1/4 cup (2 fl oz/ 60 ml) coconut milk.

Preheat the oven to 200°F (95°C).

Heat a large frying pan over medium heat until a few drops of water sprinkled on the pan immediately form beads that dance across the surface. Add 1 or 2 teaspoons oil, tilt the pan to coat the bottom, and wipe off the excess with several layers of paper towels. Using a 1/4-cup (2-fl oz/60-ml) measure, ladle the batter into the pan; try to leave about 1/2-inch between each pancake. Cook the pancakes until large bubbles appear on the tops and the bottoms are lightly browned, about 4 minutes. Turn and cook until browned on the second side, about 1 minute longer. Transfer to a plate, cover loosely with aluminum foil, and keep warm in the oven. Cook the remaining pancakes, using additional oil if necessary. You should have 12 pancakes.

In a frying pan over medium-high heat, melt the butter. When the butter is almost sizzling, add the bananas and cook, stirring occasionally, until lightly browned, about 1 minute. Sprinkle the brown sugar over the bananas and gently shake the pan until the sugar is dissolved. Stir in the lime juice.

Place 1 banana piece on each pancake and roll the pancake around the banana. Arrange 2 rolls on each plate, spoon some of the pan juices on top, sprinkle with the toasted coconut, and serve hot.

Serves 6

1 cup (5 oz/155 g) all-purpose (plain) flour

1/4 cup (2 oz/60 g) granulated sugar

2 tablespoons unsweetened shredded dried coconut

1 teaspoon baking powder

1/4 teaspoon salt

1 small ripe banana, mashed

1 egg, lightly beaten

1 3/4–2 cups (14–16 fl oz/ 430–500 ml) unsweetened coconut milk

3 tablespoons vegetable oil, or more if needed

1 1/4 cup (10 oz/310 g) unsalted butter

3 large bananas, halved lengthwise, then each half cut crosswise in half

6 tablespoons (2 1/2 oz/75 g) lightly packed golden brown sugar

6 tablespoons (3 fl oz/90 ml) lime juice

2 tablespoons unsweetened toasted flaked coconut

Mixed Berry Shortcakes

3–4 cups (12–16 oz/375–500 g) mixed berries such as strawberries, raspberries, blueberries, and blackberries in any combination

1/4 cup (2 oz/60 g) granulated sugar, plus 2 tablespoons

1 cup (4 oz/125 g) cake (soft-wheat) flour, plus flour for dusting

1/4 teaspoon salt

1 teaspoon baking powder

1 orange

1 1/2 cups (12 fl oz/375 ml) heavy (double) cream

1/2 cup sour cream

2 tablespoons confectioners' (icing) sugar

1 teaspoon vanilla extract (essence)

Position a rack in the middle of the oven and preheat the oven to 400°F (200°C).

Wash the berries and shake dry in a colander. If using strawberries, cut them into halves or quarters. Cut about one-fourth of any other berries in half. Put all the berries in a bowl and add the 1/4 cup (2 oz/60 g) granulated sugar. Toss well. Cover and refrigerate for at least 30–40 minutes or up to 1 1/2 hours.

In a bowl, stir together the cake flour, the 2 tablespoons granulated sugar, the salt, and baking powder. Set aside.

Using the small holes of a box grater grater-shredder, grate the zest from the orange over a bowl. Be sure to include all the zest clinging to the grater. Add 1/2 cup (4 fl oz/125 ml) of the cream to the zest, mixing well, and then stir into the flour mixture just until it holds together. Gather into a ball and place on a floured work surface. With floured hands knead the mixture a few times until a soft dough forms, then roll or pat out with your hands, into a 6-inch (15-cm) square. Cut the dough square into 4 pieces, each 3 inches (7.5 cm) square. Place on an ungreased baking sheet. Bake until golden and crisp, 20–25 minutes. Let cool on the baking sheet.

In a bowl, combine the remaining 1 cup (8 fl oz/250 ml) cream and the sour cream and, using a whisk or electric or hand beater, beat until just beginning to thicken. Add the confectioners' sugar and vanilla and continue to beat until soft peaks form. Cover and refrigerate until ready to serve.

Split the shortcakes in half horizontally and place the bottom halves on individual plates, cut sides up. Spoon some of the berries, with their juices, evenly over the bottoms. Place the tops on them, cut sides down. Spoon on more berries and then the whipped cream. Serve at once.

Serves 4

Nectarine and Peach Gratin with Cinnamon Sabayon

Any combination of ripe fruits, particularly the juicy varieties of summer, will marry well with this French-inspired cinnamon and orange sabayon. Be sure to cook the egg mixture over simmering—not boiling—water, or the consistency will become firm.

In a large bowl, toss together the peaches, nectarines, and blueberries. Divide the fruit evenly among six 1-cup (8-fl oz/250-ml) gratin dishes and place on a baking sheet. Preheat the broiler (grill).

Pour water to a depth of 3 inches (7.5 cm) into a saucepan and bring to a gentle simmer over medium-low heat.

Meanwhile, in a heatproof bowl, whisk together the wine, honey, eggs, orange zest, and cinnamon. Place the bowl over (but not touching) the barely simmering water in the pan. Whisk constantly until the egg mixture triples in volume and is thick and foamy, about 8 minutes. Remove from the heat and spoon over the fruit to cover completely.

Broil (grill) about 4 inches (10 cm) from the heat source until golden, about 3 minutes. Remove from the broiler and serve at once.

Serves 6

3 large peaches, halved, pitted, and each cut into 12 wedges

3 large nectarines, halved, pitted, and each cut into 8 wedges

1 cup (4 oz/125 g) blueberries

3/4 cup (6 fl oz/180 ml) sweet Muscat wine

3 tablespoons honey

3 eggs

1 tablespoon minced orange zest

3/4 teaspoon ground cinnamon

Cherry Clafouti

To ensure success with this recipe, select ripe, dark cherries. It is also best to remove their pits with a cherry pitter; if they are cut with a knife, too much juice can be released into the batter. Frozen cherries would make a fine substitute as well.

1 lb (500 g) fresh dark sweet cherries, such as Bing or Lambert

1 cup (8 fl oz/250 ml) whole milk

¼ cup (2 fl oz/60 ml) heavy (double) cream

½ cup (1½ oz/45 g) sifted cake (soft-wheat) flour

4 eggs, at room temperature

½ cup (4 oz/125 g) granulated sugar

⅛ teaspoon salt

1 tablespoon kirsch, or 1 teaspoon pure almond extract (essence)

Confectioners' (icing) sugar for dusting

Fresh mint leaves for garnish

Position a rack in the upper third of the oven and preheat to 350°F (180°C). Butter a 1½-qt (1.5-l) round, oval, or rectangular baking dish with low sides. A 10-inch (25-cm) round pie dish with sides 2 inches (5 cm) deep is a good choice.

Using a cherry pitter, pit the cherries. Arrange the cherries in a prepared baking dish in a single layer. They should just cover the bottom of the dish. Set aside.

In a saucepan over medium low heat, combine the milk and cream and heat until small bubbles appear around the edges of the pan; do not let boil. Remove from the heat and vigorously whisk in the flour, a little at a time, until well blended and no lumps remain. Set aside.

In a bowl, combine the eggs, granulated sugar, and salt and whisk until light and creamy. Add the flour mixture and the kirsch to make the batter and whisk until well blended and smooth.

Pour the batter over the cherries; it should just cover them. Place the baking dish on a baking sheet and place in the oven. Bake until browned and puffed yet still soft in the center and a sharp, thin-bladed knife inserted into the center comes out almost clean, 45–55 minutes. Transfer to a wire rack to cool slightly.

Dust the top generously with confectioners' sugar. Using a large serving spoon, place 2 or 3 spoonfuls on each dessert plate. Dust with more confectioners' sugar and garnish with the mint leaves. Serve warm.

Serves 4–6

Chocolate Mousse

In France, this mousse is usually served at the table from a large glass or porcelain bowl. You can also spoon it into individual dishes for a more elegant presentation. The candied orange peel is also delicious to accompany after-dinner coffee.

In a cup, dissolve the espresso powder in 1 tablespoon boiling water, stir in the cardamom, and set aside.

Place the chocolate and butter in a heatproof bowl and set over (but not touching) 1 inch (2.5 cm) of barely simmering water in a saucepan. Let melt, stirring occasionally. When melted, add the espresso mixture and butter and stir until blended and smooth. Remove from the heat.

In another bowl, combine the egg yolks and sugar, and whisk until increased in volume and very light, 3–4 minutes. While stirring the melted chocolate with a wooden spoon or rubber spatula, gradually add the beaten yolk mixture, then beat until the chocolate is thickened.

Place the egg whites and cream of tartar in a clean, dry bowl. Using a clean whisk or electric mixer with clean beaters, beat until stiff peaks form that hold their shape but are not dry. Add about one-fourth of the beaten whites to the chocolate mixture and, using a rubber spatula, fold gently to blend. Then, gently fold in the egg whites just until incorporated. Pour into a serving bowl. Cover the bowl with paper towels (this absorbs any condensation that forms); make sure the towels do not touch the mousse. Refrigerate for several hours until well set.

At the table, spoon the mousse into shallow dessert bowls or deep dessert plates. Place several strips of Candied Orange Peel alongside each serving. Serve at once. Pass the rest in a bowl at the table.

Serves 4

1/2 teaspoon instant espresso powder

1/8 teaspoon ground cardamom

4 oz (125 g) bittersweet chocolate, preferably a dark, rich chocolate, broken or chopped into small pieces

2 tablespoons unsalted butter, at room temperature

4 eggs, separated

1 tablespoon sugar

1/8 teaspoon cream of tartar

1 cup Candied Orange Peel (page 272)

Pear Tart with Walnuts

FOR THE TART SHELL:

1 cup (5 oz/155 g) all-purpose (plain) flour

¹/₂ cup (2 oz/60 g) cake (soft-wheat) flour

1 tablespoon sugar plus 1¹/₂ cups (12 oz/375 g)

¹/₄ teaspoon salt

¹/₂ cup (4 oz/125 g) cold unsalted butter cut into small cubes

3 firm but ripe pears such as Comice or Bosc, peeled, halved, cored, and tossed in a bowl with the juice of 1 lemon

¹/₂ cup (5 oz/155 g) apricot preserves, forced through a sieve

1 cup (4 oz/125 g) walnut pieces

Whipped cream for serving

Position a rack in the lower third of the oven and preheat to 400°F (200°C).

to make the tart shell, in a bowl, mix together the flours, the 1 tablespoon sugar, and the salt. Using a pastry blender or your fingertips, cut the butter into the flour mixture until it resembles coarse meal. Tossing the mixture with a fork, slowly add 2–3 tablespoons ice water just until the mixture holds together. Gather the dough into a ball, flatten into a round, and place between 2 pieces of plastic wrap. Roll out into a round 12 inches (30 cm) in diameter. Peel off the top sheet of plastic wrap. Invert the dough round over a 9-inch (23-cm) fluted tart pan with a removable bottom. Peel off the other piece of plastic wrap and fit the dough in the pan. Cut off the excess dough even with the rim. Refrigerate for at least 1 hour.

In a deep frying pan over medium heat, combine 3 cups (24 fl oz/750 ml) cold water and the 1¹/₂ cups (12 oz/375 g) sugar. Bring to a boil and stir to dissolve the sugar. Add the pears and lemon juice and return to a simmer; add water as needed just to cover the pears. Reduce the heat to medium-low and simmer, turning once, until the pears are almost tender, about 15 minutes. Transfer the pears to a rack placed over a baking pan and let cool.

Spread most of the preserves over the bottom of the tart shell. Cut each pear half crosswise into thin slices, keeping them together. Transfer the pears to the shell with the stem ends facing center. Brush with the remaining preserves. Fill the spaces between them with the walnuts.

Bake until the crust is golden, 1–1¹/₄ hours. Let cool on a wire rack, then remove the outer ring and slide the tart onto a flat plate. Serve warm or at room temperature with the whipped cream.

Serves 4

Mixed Berries with Zabaglione

If using strawberries cut them into halves or quarters. Place all of the berries in a bowl and toss to mix. Sprinkle with ¹/₄ cup (2 fl oz/60 ml) of the wine and toss with the 3 tablespoons sugar. Cover and refrigerate until chilled, about 1 hour, tossing carefully every 20–25 minutes.

Using the small holes of a box grater-shredder, grate the zest from the lemon over the saucer. Be sure to include all the zest clinging to the grater. You should have about 1 teaspoon zest. Set aside. Have ready a large bowl of ice cubes with a little water added.

In a heatproof bowl, or in the top pan of a double boiler, combine the egg yolks and the ¹/₃ cup (3 oz/90 g) sugar. Using a whisk, beat until light colored and creamy, 2–3 minutes. Add the remaining ¹/₂ cup (4 fl oz/125 ml) wine and whisk until well blended. Place the bowl over (but not touching) a pan of simmering water. Whisk continuously, scraping the bottom and sides of the bowl each time until the mixture has tripled in volume and is quite thick and creamy; the top should stand in soft folds. This will take 10–15 minutes; be careful that the mixture does not get too hot, or it will curdle. Quickly nest the bowl on the bowl of ice and whisk until the mixture is cold, 15–25 minutes; be sure to scrape the bottom and sides often.

In a separate bowl, using a clean whisk or an electric mixer, whip the cream until stiff peaks form. Stir in the lemon zest. Then, using a rubber spatula, fold the cream into the egg mixture until thoroughly combined. Use immediately, or cover and refrigerate for 2–3 hours; stir well before serving.

To serve, spoon the berries into bowls and top generously with the zabaglione. Sprinkle a little cinnamon on top and garnish with the mint leaves.

Serves 6

6 cups (1¹/₂ lb/750 g) ripe berries such as strawberries raspberries, and blueberries, in any combination

³/₄ cup (6 fl oz/185 ml) dry white wine

3 tablespoons sugar, plus ¹/₃ cup (3 oz/90 g)

1 lemon

4 egg yolks

¹/₂ cup (4 fl oz/125 ml) heavy (double) cream

Ground cinnamon for sprinkling

Fresh mint leaves for garnish

Beverages

Once you have decided on the nature of the meal, you can concentrate on the details of the menu itself. Here are some unique ways to add a little something special.

Sparkling Limeade

Serve this refreshing limeade when you need a change from the ubiquitous lemonade. Garnish with a slice or two of lime or kiwifruit in place of the mint sprigs, if desired.

½ cup (4 fl oz/125 ml) water

½ cup (4 oz/125 g) sugar

2 cups (16 fl oz/500 ml) fresh lime juice (from about 14 large limes)

4 cups (32 fl oz/1 l) sparkling water or club soda, chilled

4 fresh mint sprigs, plus 6 sprigs for garnish (optional)

Ice cubes

In a small saucepan over high heat, combine the water and sugar. Bring to a boil, stirring to dissolve the sugar. Boil for 1 minute. Remove from the heat and let cool.

In a large glass pitcher, stir together the sugar water and the lime juice. Cover and refrigerate until the mixture is well chilled.

Add the sparkling water or club soda to the pitcher and stir to mix well. Add 4 mint sprigs. Pour over ice cubes and decorate each glass with a mint sprig, if desired. Serve immediately.

Serves 6

Summertime Confetti Punch

This thirst-quenching drink is perfect for a midafternoon treat. Serve on a warm summer day with or between meals.

1½ cups (12 fl oz/375 ml) orange juice

1 can (2fl oz/1.4 l) unsweetened pineapple juice

1 bottle (32 fl oz/1 l) cranberry–apple drink

1 bottle (24 fl oz/750 ml) grape juice

¼ cup (2 oz/ 60 g) granulated sugar

¼ cup (2 fl oz/60 ml) water

⅓ cup (3 fl oz/80 ml) fresh lemon juice

1 bottle (32 fl oz/1 l) sparkling water

Fill ice-cube trays with the orange juice, pineapple juice, cranberry-apple drink, and grape juice. Do not mix the juices in the compartments, and make an equal number of cubes of each different juice. Put the ice-cube trays in the freezer until the juice cubes are frozen solid. Refrigerate the remaining pineapple, cranberry-apple, and grape juices.

In a small saucepan over high heat, combine the sugar and water. Cook, stirring constantly with a wooden spoon, until the sugar dissolves, about 1 minute. Continue cooking without stirring until the mixture comes to a boil. Boil for 1 minute. Remove from the heat, and let cool.

Put the lemon juice in a punch bowl. Add the cooled sugar water and the remaining pineapple, cranberry-apple, and grape juices. Add the sparkling water and stir to mix well. Add the frozen juice cubes to the punch.

Ladle the punch into individual cups. Make sure each serving gets different-colored juice cubes. Serve at once.

Serves 12

Iced Tea Cooler

Tangy and refreshing, this cooler is partially made in advance. The ginger ale, however, must be added just before serving, so be sure it is well chilled.

4 cups (32 fl oz/1 l) brewed black tea, cooled

1 cup (8 fl oz/250 ml) orange juice

1 cup (8 fl oz/250 ml) cranberry juice

2½ tablespoons fresh lemon juice, or more to taste

4 teaspoons superfine (caster) sugar, or more to taste

3 cups (24 fl oz/750 ml) ginger ale, well chilled

Ice cubes

3 orange slices, halved

In a large glass pitcher, combine the tea, orange juice, cranberry juice, 2½ tablespoons lemon juice, and 4 teaspoons sugar. Mix well. Cover and refrigerate until well chilled.

Just before serving, stir in the ginger ale. Taste for sweetness, adding more lemon juice or sugar if needed. Pour over ice cubes in tall glasses. Cut a slit in each halve orange slice and rest on the glass rim to decorate. Serve at once.

Serves 6

Vietnamese Iced Coffee

This drink, for those who like their coffee sweet and strong, is served during and after meals. You need a special filter device made for this purpose, available at Asian markets.

1 cup (8 fl oz/250 ml) water

3 tablespoons sweetened condensed milk, or to taste

3 tablespoons dark-roast medium-grind French coffee

Ice cubes

In a teakettle or saucepan, bring the water to a boil. Pour the condensed milk into a heatproof 8-fl oz (250-ml) glass that is about 3½ inches (9 cm) wide at the top. Spoon the ground coffee into the filter and screw the filter on tightly. Set the filter on top of the glass.

Spoon 2 tablespoons of the boiling water into the top filter to moisten the ground coffee. Allow the coffee to absorb the water for about 30 seconds. Bring the coffee filter and glass and the remaining boiling water to the table. Slowly pour the water into the filter and allow the coffee to slowly drip until all the water is used, about 10 minutes. Add ice cubes and more milk, if desired. Serve cold.

Serves 1

Bloody Mary

Simply omit the vodka to transform this brunch classic into a delicious Virgin Mary.

2½ cups (20 fl oz/625 ml) tomato juice, well chilled

2½ cups (20 fl oz/625 ml) vegetable juice cocktail such as V8 juice or Snappy Tom, well chilled

1½ cups (12 fl oz/375 ml) vodka

¼ cup (2 fl oz/60 ml) fresh lime juice

2 teaspoons Worcestershire sauce

½ teaspoon hot-pepper sauce

Salt and freshly ground black pepper to taste

Ice cubes

6 celery ribs with leaves

In a pitcher, whisk together the tomato juice, vegetable juice cocktail, vodka, lime juice, and Worcestershire and hot-pepper sauces. Season with salt and black pepper. Taste and adjust the seasonings.

Fill another pitcher with ice cubes, add the tomato juice mixture, and stir well. Strain into glasses and garnish with the celery ribs.

Serves 6

Basic Recipes

These basic recipes and techniques are used throughout Casual Entertaining. Once you have mastered them, you'll turn to them again and again to create delicious meals.

Beef Stock

Making stock at home is an all-day task, but the results are well worth the time. You can prepare a large batch of stock and freeze it in small containers for future use.

6 lb (3 kg) meaty beef shanks

Beef scraps or other trimmings, if available

2 onions, coarsely chopped

1 leek, trimmed, carefully washed, and coarsely chopped

2 carrots, peeled and coarsely chopped

1 celery rib, coarsely chopped

Mushroom stems (optional)

6 cloves garlic

4 fresh flat-leaf (Italian) parsley sprigs

10 whole peppercorns

3 fresh thyme sprigs

2 small bay leaves

Preheat the oven to 450°F (220°C). Place the beef shanks in a large roasting pan and roast, turning occasionally, until browned but not burned, about 1 1/2 hours.

Transfer the browned shanks to a large stockpot, reserving the juices in the pan, and add cold water to cover by 2 inches. Add the beef scraps, if using. Bring to a boil over medium-high heat. Reduce the heat to low and simmer, uncovered, for 2 hours. While the stock simmers, using a large spoon, skim off any scum and froth that forms on the surface. Add water as needed to keep the bones generously immersed.

Meanwhile, place the roasting pan on the stove top. Add the onions, leek, carrots, and celery to the fat remaining in the pan. Brown over high heat, stirring often, until the vegetables caramelize but are not scorched, 15–20 minutes.

When the shanks have simmered for 2 hours, add the browned vegetables to the stockpot. Pour 1 cup (8 fl oz/250 ml) hot water into the roasting pan, bring to a simmer, and deglaze the pan by stirring to dislodge any browned bits from the bottom. Add these juices to the stockpot.

Place the mushroom stems (if using), garlic, parsley, peppercorns, thyme, and bay leaves on a small square of cheesecloth (muslin) and tie with kitchen string into a small bag. Add to the stockpot. Simmer, over low heat, uncovered, for 6 hours longer (for a total of 8 hours).

Remove from the heat and remove the solids with a slotted spoon or skimmer. Strain the stock through a fine-mesh sieve lined with cheesecloth (muslin) into a clean pot (if using the stock immediately) or storage container (if saving the stock for future use). If using immediately, use a large spoon to skim the fat from the surface of the stock. Discard the fat and use the stock in the desired recipe.

If storing the stock, let it cool to room temperature, then cover tightly and refrigerate for up to 5 days, or freeze for up to 6 months. Before using the stock, remove the solidified fat that sits on top of the stock.

Makes 4–5 qt (4–5 l)

Chicken Stock

Any type of chicken can be used for making this stock, although pieces of a stewing chicken will yield the most flavor. Be sure to cut the chicken into small pieces.

2 1/2 lb (1.25 kg) chicken pieces, including bones

4 celery ribs with leaves, coarsely chopped

2 carrots, peeled and coarsely chopped

2 yellow onions, coarsely chopped

2 leeks, white part only, carefully washed and coarsely chopped

Bouquet garni (page 289)

Put the chicken pieces into a large stockpot and add cold water to cover by at least 2 inches. Bring to a boil over medium-high heat. Reduce the heat to low and simmer for about 30 minutes. While the stock simmers, using a large spoon, skim off any scum on the surface.

Add the celery, carrots, onions, leeks, and bouquet garni. Cover partially and boil gently for 30 minutes longer; check periodically, skimming off any scum that forms on the surface.

Remove the stock pot from the heat and remove the solids with a slotted spoon or skimmer. Carefully strain the stock through a fine-mesh sieve lined with cheesecloth (muslin) into a clean pot (if using the stock immediately) or storage container (if saving the stock for future use). If using the stock right away, use a large spoon to skim the fat from the surface of the stock. Discard the fat and use the stock as directed in the desired recipe.

If storing the stock, let it cool to room temperature, then cover tightly and refrigerate for up to 5 days, or freeze for up to 6 months. Before using the stock, remove the solidified fat that sits on top of the stock.

Makes about 5 cups (40 fl oz/1.25 l)

Vegetable Stock

Sautéing the vegetables before adding water gives this particular stock a special depth of flavor.

2 tablespoons vegetable oil

2 large onions, coarsely chopped

4 celery ribs with leaves, coarsely chopped

3 carrots, peeled and coarsely chopped

1 green bell pepper (capsicum), seeded, deribbed, and coarsely chopped

1 teaspoon salt

Bouquet garni (page 316)

In a large stockpot over medium heat, warm the vegetable oil. Add the onions, celery, carrots, and bell pepper and sauté, stirring often, until the onions are translucent, and other vegtables are tender, about 10 minutes.

Add 10 cups (2 1/2 qt/2.5 l) water, the salt, and the bouquet garni. Bring to a boil over medium-high heat. Reduce the heat to low and simmer for 30 minutes.

Remove the stock pot from the heat and remove the solids with a slotted spoon or skimmer. Strain the stock through a fine-mesh sieve lined with cheesecloth (muslin) into a clean pot (if using the stock immediately) or storage container (if saving it for future use).

If using the stock immediately, proceed with the desired recipe.

If storing the stock, let it cool to room temperature, then cover tightly and refrigerate for up to 5 days, or freeze for up to 12 months.

Makes about 8 cups (64 fl oz/2 l)

Bouquet Garni

1 bay leaf

6 whole peppercorns

1 clove garlic, sliced

3 fresh flat-leaf (Italian) parsley sprigs

Cut out a 6-inch (15-cm) square of the cheesecloth (muslin). Place the bay leaf, peppercorns, garlic, and parsley sprigs in the center of the cheesecloth, bring the corners together, and tie securely with kitchen string. Use as directed in individual recipes.

Makes 1 sachet

Fresh Egg Pasta

2 1/4 cups (11 1/2 oz/360 g) all-purpose (plain) flour, plus flour as needed

3 eggs, lightly beaten

Semolina flour for dusting

Place 2 1/4 cups (11 1/2 oz/360 g) flour in a mound on a work surface. Make a well in the center and pour the beaten eggs into the well. Using a fork, gradually incorporate the flour from the sides of the well, taking care not to break the flour wall. Continue working in more flour until the dough is no longer wet.

Begin kneading the dough by hand, adding additional flour if needed, until the dough is smooth and no longer sticky, 2–3 minutes. Reserve the remaining flour.

Dust several baking sheets with semolina flour. Divide the dough in half on the work surface and cover with a kitchen towel to prevent drying. Set up your pasta machine alongside another work surface with some of the reserved flour. Using a rolling pin, flatten the first dough half into a rectangle thin enough to go through the rollers at the widest setting.

Pass the dough through the rollers once then lay it down on the work surface and flour it lightly. Fold into thirds lengthwise to make a rectangular shape and flour both sides lightly. Flatten the dough with the rolling pin until it is thin enough to go through the rollers again. With one of the two open edges going first, pass the dough through the rollers nine more times at the widest setting; after each time, flour, fold, and flatten the dough as described. After 10 trips through the wide rollers the dough should be completely smooth and supple.

Starting at the second-to-widest setting, pass the dough through the rollers repeatedly, setting the rollers one notch narrower each time. When the pasta length gets unwieldy, cut it

in half and continue rolling one part at a time until the dough reaches the desired thinness.

Arrange the finished pasta sheets on the prepared baking sheets and cover with kitchen towels to prevent drying. Repeat the entire process with the second half of dough. Cut the pasta by hand or machine if desired.

Makes 1 lb (500 g) dough

Fresh Spinach Pasta

Adding fresh spinach lends a chewier texture, greater flavor, and vibrant color to the classic egg pasta dough.

1 lb (500 g) fresh spinach, tough stems removed

2 eggs

About 3 cups (15 oz/470 g) all-purpose (plain) flour

Semolina flour for dusting

Rinse the spinach well, drain, and place in a large frying pan. Cover and cook over medium heat until the spinach wilts, 2–3 minutes. Drain in a sieve under cold running water. When cool, squeeze thoroughly dry.

Place the spinach in a food processor with 1 of the eggs. Process to a smooth puree, stopping once or twice to scrape down the sides.

Make the pasta dough as you would for the Fresh Egg Pasta (page 289), putting the spinach mixture and the remaining egg, lightly beaten, into

the well of flour to make the dough. When fully incorporated, knead and roll out the pasta dough as directed in Fresh Egg Pasta.

Makes 1 1/2 lb (750 g) dough

Classic Tomato Sauce

This tomato sauce is marvelous with all fresh pastas especially rigatoni and fettuccini. If using fresh tomatoes, make sure that they are the ripest and best quality you can find, and use only fresh basil, which is more aromatic than the dried herb. If the tomatoes' flavor is a bit acidic, add a tiny spoonful of sugar to perk them up. The butter in this recipe is typical of northern Italian cooking; but feel free to substitute olive oil, if you wish.

1/4 cup (3 oz/90 g) unsalted butter

1 small white onion, thinly sliced crosswise

1 lb (500 g) fresh plum (Roma) tomatoes, peeled, seeded, and sliced lengthwise, or canned plum tomatoes, drained and chopped

Salt and freshly ground black pepper

8 fresh basil leaves, torn into small pieces

In a large frying pan over medium heat, melt the butter. Add the onion and about 3 tablespoons water, cover the pan, and cook gently, stirring occasionally, until tender and translucent, about 10 minutes.

Add the tomatoes, cover partially, and continue to cook over low heat until a thick and creamy, about 20 minutes. If the sauce begins to dry out too much, add a few tablespoons water to the pan.

Add the salt and pepper to taste and the basil and stir well. Remove from the heat and let stand, covered, for a few minutes to allow the flavors to marry.

Serves 4

Basic Pizza Dough

1½ cups (7½ oz/235 g) all-purpose (plain) flour, plus up to 1 tablespoon, if needed, plus flour for dusting

2½ teaspoons (1 package) quick-rise active dry yeast

½ teaspoon salt

½ teaspoon sugar

1 tablespoon olive oil

To make the dough, in a food processor, combine the 1½ cups (7½ oz/235 g) flour, yeast, salt, and sugar. Process briefly to mix. With the motor running, pour in ½ cup (4 fl oz/125 ml) warm water (115°–125°F/46°–52°C) and the olive oil in a steady stream, processing until the dough forms a ball. If it seems too wet, add up to 1 tablespoon flour; if it is too dry, add up to 1 tablespoon warm water. Transfer the dough to a lightly floured work surface and knead a few times to form a smooth ball. Place the dough in an oiled bowl, cover, and let rise in a warm place until almost doubled in bulk, 45–60 minutes.

Poached Eggs

⅓ cup (3 fl oz/80 ml) distilled white vinegar

8 eggs

1 tablespoon salt

In a large sauté pan over high heat, combine the 4qt (4 l) water, vinegar, and salt and bring to a boil. Reduce the heat to just under a boil. One at a time, crack the eggs and slip them into the simmering water. After all the eggs are added, reduce the heat to a gentle simmer. Cook until the whites are set and the yolks are glazed over but still liquid, about 3 minutes. Using a slotted spoon, transfer the eggs to a kitchen towel to drain. Trim off any streamers of egg white.

Basic Tart Dough

1½ cups (7½ oz/235 g) all-purpose (plain) flour

Pinch of salt

½ cup (4 oz/125 g) chilled unsalted butter, cut into pieces

In a food processor, combine the flour and salt and pulse to combine. Add the butter and process until the mixture resembles cornmeal. Add 3 tablespoons ice water and process until the dough just holds together, adding an additional 1 tablespoon ice water if the mixture is too dry. Gather the dough into a ball, place in plastic wrap, and refrigerate for at least 1 hour or for up to 3 days.

Makes one 9-inch (23-cm) tart shell

Lemon Curd

2 or 3 lemons

½ cup (4 oz/125 g) sugar

3 eggs

½ cup (4 oz/125 g) unsalted butter, cut into small cubes

Using the fine-holes on a box grater-shredder, grate the zest from 1 lemon. Cut each lemon in half and squeeze enough juice to measure ⅓ cup (3 fl oz/80 ml).

In a heavy, nonreactive saucepan, combine the lemon juice and zest, sugar, and eggs. Whisk until well blended. Place over medium-low heat. Stirring constantly, add the butter, letting the cubes melt before adding more and scraping the bottom of the pan each time. Cook slowly, stirring continuously, until thickened, 10–15 minutes. The curd should be smooth and free of lumps.

Transfer the curd to a bowl and cover with plastic wrap, pressing the wrap directly onto the surface of the curd. Set aside to cool. The curd can be stored tightly covered in the refrigerator for up to 1 week.

Makes 1½ cups (12 fl oz/375 ml)

Glossary

Anchovies Indigenous to the Mediterranean and the Atlantic coastlines of Spain and Portugal, anchovies are used widely in the cuisines of those countries, as well as in Italy and southern France. When added to a dish during cooking, the anchovies will virtually dissolve, and leave only their surprisingly subtle, nonfishy dimension of flavor. They are generally packed in oil and are drained before using.

Artichoke This vegetable is actually the flower bud harvested from a plant of the thistle family. Baby artichokes are not young artichokes, but rather smaller ones that grow lower on the plant. All artichokes have a mild, nutty flavor. Choose ones heavy for their size, with tightly closed leaves.

Asparagus These tall, tender-crisp spears can be as thin as a pencil or as thick as your thumb. Look for firm stalks with tightly closed tips.

Avocado Rich in flavor and texture, avocados are most commonly found in two varieties: California's dark green, dimpled Hass avocado and the smoother, paler green Fuerte. Hass avocados boast the highest oil content and will produce the best results in guacamole.

Bok Choy Also known as Shanghai bok choy, pale green, tender baby bok choy has a flavor somewhere between celery and cabbage. Give particular attention to the base when cleaning, as grit is often lodged between the stems and should be rinsed thourghly.

Broth & Stock Commercially produced, well-flavored liquids made by cooking meat, poultry, fish, or vegetables in water. Canned broths tend to be saltier than homemade, so seek out a high-quality brand that offers a "low-sodium" or "reduced-sodium" product for better control of the seasoning in your dish. You can also purchase excellent "homemade" stocks in fresh or frozen quantities from upscale supermarkets and specialty-food stores.

Buttermilk Made by adding bacteria to skimmed milk to convert sugars to acid, buttermilk is slightly thick and tangy.

Capers The small unopened flower buds of bushes native to the Mediterranean, capers are dried, cured, and then usually packed in a vinegar brine or in salt. Rinse them and blot dry before using.

Cheeses A good cheese shop is a rewarding experience, since you'll be able to taste a variety of types before you buy. Store cheeses in a warmer part of the refrigerator, like the door, wrapped in parchment (baking) or waxed paper rather than plastic, to allow them to breathe.

Fontina A mild, fruity Italian cow's milk cheese with a pleasing firmness and light but heady aroma.

Feta A young cheese traditionally made from sheep's milk and known for its crumbly texture. Feta's saltiness is heightened by the brine in which the cheese is packed.

Gorgonzola This cow's-milk blue cheese from Italy has a moist, creamy texture and complex flavor.

Gruyère This pungent semi firm, dense, and smooth cow's milk cheese is produced in Switzerland and France and is appreciated for its mild, slightly tangy favor and superior melting properties.

Manchego A Spanish sheep's-milk cheese with a mild, pale yellow interior dotted with holes and a mild and slightly salty taste.

Mozzarella A mild, creamy cheese made from cow's or water buffalo's milk curd formed into balls. If at all possible, seek out fresh mozzarella, which is sold surrounded by a little of the whey, rather than the rubbery products made in large factories.

Parmigiano-Reggiano This firm, aged, salty cheese is made from partially skimmed cow's milk. It has a rich, nutty flavor and a pleasant, granular texture and is the most renowned of all Parmesan cheeses.

Provolone Made from cow's milk, provolone is sold in young and aged versions. Both are smooth, dense, and lightly salty, and have almost a buttery essence; the latter is more bold with a spicier, sharper taste, is harder, and is used for grating.

Chile Powder A pure powder made by grinding a single specific variety of dried chile. Ancho and New Mexico chile powders are the most common. Seek out chipotle chile powder for a particularly smoky flavor. Be careful not to confuse chile powder with chili powder, typically a blend of powdered dried chile, oregano, cumin, and other seasonings.

Chili Sauce Not to be confused with the many Asian chile sauces, this American-style sauce is a mild, ketchuplike blend of tomatoes, chili powder, onions, green bell peppers (capsicums), vinegar, sugar, and spices. Look for chili sauce near the condiments in the supermarket.

Chorizo Coarsely ground spicy pork sausage used in Mexican and Spanish cooking. It's best to remove the casings before cooking.

Cornstarch This highly refined, silky powder, also referred to as cornflour, which is made from corn kernels and is most commonly used as a thicking agent in sauces. It has nearly twice the thickening power of flour and gives sauces a glossy sheen,

Chiles

Fresh chiles range in size from tiny to large, and in heat intensity from mild to fiery hot. Select firm, bright-colored chiles with blemish-free skins. To reduce the heat of a chile, remove the ribs and seeds, where the heat-producing compound, called capsaicin, resides. When working with hot chiles, wear a latex glove to avoid burning your skin, then wash your hands and any utensils thoroughly with hot, soapy water the moment you finish.

Anaheim Classically used for chiles rellenos, anaheims have a tough skin and are often roasted or charred before using. They also are chiles you find cooked and chopped in cans labeled "green chiles." Use them in place of poblanos. When dried, anaheims are typically called California chiles.

Ancho A mild, dark reddish brown or brick red, squat looking dried poblano chile. About 4 inches (10 cm) long, anchos have a nice heat along with their natural sweetness.

Arbol About 3 inches (7.5 cm) long, narrow, and very hot. These chiles are bright orange when fresh and red to orange when dried.

Chipotle A dried and smoked jalapeño chile, with lots of flavor and lots of heat. These dark brown chiles are about 3 inches (7.5 cm) long and

are sold either dried whole or ground, or packed in an onion-y tomato mixture called adobo sauce.

Jalapeño Ranging from mildly hot to fiery, this fleshy chile is usually green but also can be red. The fresh hot chile measures 2–4 inches (5–10 cm) long. Green jalapeños are widely available in supermarkets.

Poblano Large and fairly mild, the fresh, dark green poblano is about 5 inches (13 cm) long and has broad "shoulders." Poblano chiles, which are usually roasted and peeled, have a nutty flavor and are often stuffed and fried for chile rellenos. When dried, these chiles are called ancho chiles. The drying process turns them a dark reddish-brown color.

Serrano Similar to a jalapeño chile in heat intensity, the serrano chile is sleeker and tends to have more consistent heat than its cousin. Approximately 2 inches (5 cm) long, serranos can be found in green or red form (the red ones are ripe versions of the green) and can be used in place of jalapeños in any recipe. Although they are the most often available fresh in most produce stores, occasionally you may find dried serranos secos.

unlike the opaque finish of a flour-thickened sauce.

Coconut Milk Rich and nutty flavored and made by soaking grated coconut in water, coconut milk is an essential ingredient throughout the tropics. It thickens sauces, turns rice dishes creamy, flavors desserts, smooths out soups, and is the perfect foil for the heat of chiles. Unsweetened coconut milk should not be confused with canned sweetened coconut cream, sometimes labeled "cream of coconut," which is used primarily for desserts and tropical drinks.

Cucumber, English Also known as hothouse cucumbers, these cucumbers can grow up to 2 feet (60 cm) long. They are nearly seedless, which makes them a popular choice for soups and salads.

Curry Powder Typical ingredients in this ground spice blend from South Asia include turmeric, cumin, coriander, pepper, cardamom, mustard, cloves, and ginger. Curry powders are categorized as mild, hot, and very hot. Madras curry powder is a well-balanced version with medium heat.

Eggplant The most familiar, globe eggplant (aubergine), is usually large, egg-or-pear shaped, with skin that looks almost black.

Fennel The stems of a fennel plant swell to overlap the base, forming a bulb with white to pale green ribbed layers that look similar to celery. Fennel is known for its mild anise flavor.

Fig, Black Mission Small and sweet, Black Mission figs are one of more that 150 fig varieties. When ripe, they should have a deep purple-black color and should feel soft, but not squishy when gently pressed.

Fish Sauce A clear liquid used in southeast Asian cooking and as a table condiment, much like soy sauce. It ranges in color from amber to dark brown and has a pungent aroma and strong salty flavor.

Garlic When buying garlic, choose plump, firm heads with no brown discoloration. (A tinge of purple is fine, even desirable.) Always take care not to cook garlic beyond a light gold, or it can taste harsh and bitter.

Ginger A refreshing combination of spicy and sweet in both aroma and flavor, ginger adds a lively note to many recipes, particularly Asian dishes. Select ginger that is firm and heavy and has a smooth skin.

Haricots Verts Also called French green bean or fillet bean. Small, slender, dark green, young pod beans favored in France. Delicately flavored, they are more elegant, and commensurately expensive, than other green beans.

Mangoes Juicy, sweet-fleshed fruit native to India and now cultivated in many other tropical regions. When shopping for ripe mangoes, choose fruits that are aromatic at their stem ends.

Mustard, Dijon Originating in Dijon, France, this silky smooth and slightly tangy mustard contains brown or black mustard seeds, white wine, and herbs.

Oil The heat requirements and other ingredients of a recipe usually suggest which oil is appropriate to use. As a general rule, choose less-refined, more flavorful oils for uncooked uses, such as tossing raw or already cooked foods, and refined, blander oils for cooking.

Asian sesame This amber-colored oil, pressed from toasted sesame seeds, has a rich, nutty flavor. Look for it in well-stocked markets and Asian groceries.

Canola This neutral-flavored oil, notable for its monounsaturated fats, is recommended for general cooking.

Grapeseed Pressed from grape seeds and mild in flavor, this all-purpose oil heats to very high temperatures without smoking, making it suitable for frying, and is also used in salad dressings and marinades.

Olive Made from the first pressing of the olives without the use of heat or chemicals, extra-virgin olive oil is clear green or brownish and has a fruity, slightly peppery flavor that is used to best advantage when it will not be cooked. In the past, such oil was labeled "pure olive oil." Today, it is usually labeled simply "olive oil."

Peanut Pressed from peanuts, this mildly fragrant oil has a nutty flavor and does not smoke at high temperatures.

Olives, Kalamata The most popular Greek variety, the Kalamata olive is almond shaped, purplish black, rich, and meaty. It is brine-cured and then packed in oil or wine.

Onions This humble bulb vegetable, in the same family as leeks and garlic, is one of the most common ingredients in the kitchen.

Green Often known as scallions or spring onions, green onions are the immature shoots of the bulb onion. They have a narrow white base that has not yet begun to swell and long, flat green leaves, also referred to as "tops." They are commonly used as garnish.

Red These onions tend to be mild, slightly sweet, and purplish. They are delicious when used raw.

Yellow These are common, all-purpose onions sold in supermarkets. They are usually too harsh to be eaten raw but become rich and sweet when cooked.

Papaya A tropical fruit with a hollow center, that holds a shiny mass of small, black edible seeds with a slightly peppery flavor.

Herbs

Using fresh herbs is one of the best things you can do to improve your cooking. Dried herbs do have their place, but fresh herbs usually bring brighter flavors to a dish.

Basil Used in kitchens throughout the Mediterranean and in Southeast Asia, fresh basil adds a highly aromatic, peppery flavor.

Chives These slender, hollow, grass-shaped blades give an onion-like flavor to dishes, without the bite.

Cilantro Also called fresh coriander or Chinese parsley, cilantro has a bright astringent taste. It is used extensively in Mexican, Asian, Indian, Latin, and Middle Eastern cuisines.

Dill This herb has fine, feathery leaves with a distinct aroma and flavor.

Lemongrass An aromatic herb used in much of Southeast Asia, lemongrass resembles a green (spring) onion in shape but has a fresh lemony aroma and flavor. Use only the pale green bottom part for cooking. Since the fibers are tough, lemongrass needs to be removed from a dish after cooking much like a bay leaf.

Marjoram A native of the Mediterranean region, marjoram has a milder, sweeter flavor than that of its cousin, oregano. It can be used fresh or dried.

Mint This refreshing herb is available in many varieties, with spearmint the most commonly found.

Oregano A distinctive and spicy herb also known as wild marjoram. It is one of the few herbs that keeps its flavor when dried.

Parsley Also known as flat-leaf parsley, this dark green Italian variety of the faintly peppery herb adds vibrant color and a pleasing flavor to a wide variety of preparations.

Rosemary This woody Mediterranean herb with leaves like pine needles, has an assertive flavor. Always use rosemary in moderation, as its flavor can overwhelm a dish if you use too much of it.

Sage The soft, gray-green leaves of this Mediterranean herb are sweet and aromatic.

Tarragon The slender, delicate, deep green leaves of tarragon impart an elegant, aniselike scent.

Winter Savory This shrub-like Mediterranean evergreen herb has a strong, spicy flavor that some cooks liken to thyme. It complements dried beans and lentils, meats, poultry, and tomatoes.

Paprika Red or orange-red, paprika is made from the flesh of dried peppers. The finest paprikas originate from Hungary and Spain and are found in three basic types: sweet, medium-sweet, and hot. Sweet paprika, which is mild but still very pungent, is the most versatile. The best Spanish paprika, commonly known as pimentón de La Vera, is made from smoked peppers, which give it a distinctive flavor.

Prosciutto A famed Italian thinly-sliced ham, cut from the rear leg of the pig, lightly seasoned, cured with salt, and then air-dried. Celebrated for its subtle but intense flavor, prosciutto is eaten raw in salads or cooked as a flavoring agent.

Radicchio
A member of the chicory family native to Italy and characterized by its variegated purplish red leaves and pleasantly bitter taste.

Red Bell Pepper Also known as sweet peppers and capsicums, these flavorful, colorful vegetables are delicious raw and especially roasted. They are typically charred and then peeled, resulting in a smoky flavor. Look for peppers that are firm, smooth, and brightly colored, with no blemishes.

Shallots These small members of the onion family look like large cloves of garlic covered with papery bronze or reddish skin. Shallots have white flesh streaked with purple, a crisp texture, and a flavor more subtle than that of onions.

Shrimp Although often sold peeled and deveined, it's best to purchase shrimp (prawns) still in their shells if possible. Most shrimp have been previously frozen, and the shells help preserve their texture and flavor.

Spices An important part of pantry, spices, used whole or ground, add flavor, aroma, and texture to marinades, rubs, and other preparations.

Aniseed The seed of the anise plant, a member of the parsley family, aniseed has a licorice taste.

Coriander The dried ripe fruit of fresh coriander, or cilantro. Its tiny, round, ridged seeds add an exotic flavor to both savory and sweet foods.

Cumin The seed of a member of the parsley family, cumin adds a sharp flavor to many Latin American and Indian dishes.

Fennel This mediterranean spice has a sweet aniselike flavor and is used to enhance the flavors in meat, chicken, and fish.

Five spice Sometimes labeled "Chinese five-spice powder" this potent spice blend varies in its makeup, but usually contains cloves, aniseeds or fennel seeds, star anise, cinnamon, Sichuan peppercorns, and sometimes ginger.

Garlic Powder Ground, dried garlic cloves used to easily add garlic essence to dishes, and rubs and marinades for meat and fish.

Nutmeg The oval brown seed of a soft fruit, nutmeg has a warm, sweet, spicy flavor. It has a hard shell that is often covered by a membrane. The membrane is separated and ground to become mace.

Onion Powder Ground, dried onion used as an all-purpose seasoning and in spice rubs.

Star Anise A dried star-shaped seedpod of a Chinese evergreen tree related to the magnolia. It is slightly more bitter than aniseed and has a distinct licorice flavor that pairs well with meats.

Turmeric Like saffron, turmeric is valued both for its taste and its bright color. The root of a plant belonging to the ginger family, turmeric is used fresh and dried.

Swiss Chard Also known as chard. A cooking green with large, crinkled leaves on fleshy, ribbed stems. There are two varieties: one with red stems and another with pearly white . Red chard, also marketed as rhubarb or ruby chard has a slightly earthier flavor, while chard with white stems tends to be sweeter.

Tomatoes Comes in a wide range of sizes, from currant tomatoes no bigger then blueberries to fat beefsteaks up to 5 inches (3 cm) in diameter. The colors vary too from white to purple-black to reddish black with green striped zebra tomatoes somewhere in between.

Cherry miniature, Sweet tomatoes available in yellow, red, and orange. Look for red sweet 100s or orange Sun golds, both especially sweet and intensely flavored.

Roma Also known as plum or egg tomatoes, these have a meaty, flavorful flesh that is particularly good for making sauce.

Vinegar Many types of vinegar are available, made from a variety of wines or, like rice vinegar, from grains. They often add just the right amount of tartness to a dish.

Balsamic This aged vinegar is made from the pure wine must–unfermented grape juice–of white Trebbiano grapes. Balsamic is aged for as little as 1 year or for as long as 75 years; the vinegar slowly evaporates and grows sweeter and mellower.

White wine A pantry staple carried in most supermarkets, white wine vinegar is created by allowing white wine to ferment naturally over a period of several months.

Worcestershire Sauce

A traditional English condiment and flavoring, Worcestershire sauce is an intensely flavored blend of varied ingredients, including molasses, soy sauce, garlic, onion, and fermented anchovies.

Mushrooms

The popularity of all types of mushrooms has resulted in the successful farming of many different varieties, blurring the distinction between cultivated and wild. Wild or farmed, mushrooms are delicious when roasted or grilled and contribute a deep earthiness to recipes.

White The cultivated, all-purpose mushroom sold in grocery stores. Sometimes called button mushrooms, although the term refers specifically to young, tender ones with closed caps. For general cooking, use the medium-sized mushrooms with little or no gills showing. The large ones are excellent for stuffing.

Cremini Closely related to the white mushroom and can be used whenever white mushrooms are called for, but they have a light brown color, firmer texture, and fuller flavor.

Morel Considered the king of all mushrooms, the morel has a strong, intense, musky flavor that makes it highly sought after. The uncultivated mushroom has a dark, elongated, spongelike cap and hollow stem. Morels are especially delicious in cream sauces and scrambled eggs, and typically used in French cuisine.

Oyster Cream to pale gray, these mushrooms have a fan shape and a subtle flavor of shellfish. They used to be wild only but are now cultivated.

Porcini Also known as ceps and bolete. Porcini (Italian for "little pigs") are indeed nicely plump, with a firm texture, sweet fragrance, and full, earthy flavor. An uncultivated variety, they have caps similar to that of cremini in shape and color, but their stems are thick and swollen. They can be difficult to find in the U.S., however, dried porcini can be used. They are excellent in soups, pasta sauces, and risotto. Thinly slice young, fresh ones and dress them with a simple vinaigrette.

Portobello A cultivated mushroom the portobello is a mature cremini mushroom. They a smoky flavor and meaty texture. The thick, tough stems should be removed before cooking.

Shiitake The most popular mushroom in Japan and is now widely cultivated. Buff to dark brown, they are available fresh and dried. Fresh shiitakes should have smooth, plump caps, while better-quality dried ones have pale cracks in the caps' surfaces. Dried shiitake and Chinese black mushrooms can be used interchangeably. Shiitake take well to grilling, roasting, stir-frying, and sautéing.

Index

First published in the USA by Time-Life Custom Publishing.

Originally published as Williams-Sonoma Lifestyle Series:
After Dinner (© 1998 Weldon Owen Inc.)
Chicken for Dinner (© 1998 Weldon Owen Inc.)
Classic Pasta at Home (© 1998 Weldon Owen Inc.)
Everyday Roasting (© 1998 Weldon Owen Inc.)
Fresh & Light (© 1998 Weldon Owen Inc.)
Holiday Celebrations (© 1998 Weldon Owen Inc.)
Soup for Supper (© 1998 Weldon Owen Inc.)
Vegetarian for All Seasons (© 1998 Weldon Owen Inc.)
Asian Flavors (© 1999 Weldon Owen Inc.)
Backyard Barbeque (© 1999 Weldon Owen Inc.)
Brunch Entertaining (© 1999 Weldon Owen Inc.)
Cooking From the Farmer's Market (© 1999 Weldon Owen Inc.)
Cooking for Yourself (© 1999 Weldon Owen Inc.)
Food & Wine Pairing (© 1999 Weldon Owen Inc.)
Holiday Cooking with Kids (© 1999 Weldon Owen Inc.)
Small Plates (© 1999 Weldon Owen Inc.)
Weekends with Friends (© 2000 Weldon Owen Inc.)

In collaboration with Williams-Sonoma Inc.
3250 Van Ness Avenue, San Francisco, CA 94109

Oxmoor House.

OXMOOR HOUSE INC.
Oxmoor House books are distributed by Sunset Books
80 Willow Road, Menlo Park, CA 94025
Telephone: 650-321-3600 Fax 650-324-1532
Vice President/General Manager: Rich Smeby
National Accounts Manager/Special Sales: Brad Moses

Oxmoor House and Sunset Books are divisions of
Southern Progress Corporation

WILLIAMS-SONOMA
Founder and Vice-Chairman: Chuck Williams

WELDON OWEN INC.
Chief Executive Officer: John Owen
President and Chief Operating Officer: Terry Newell
President and Chief Operating Officer: Christine E. Munson
Vice President International Sales: Stuart Laurence

Vice President and Creative Director: Gaye Allen
Vice President and Publisher: Hannah Rahill
Senior Designer: Kara Church
Associate Editor: Lauren Higgins
Production Director: Chris Hemesath
Production and Reprint Coordinator: Todd Rechner
Color Manager: Teri Bell

Williams-Sonoma Casual Entertaining was conceived and
produced by Weldon Owen Inc.
814 Montgomery Street, San Francisco, CA 94133
Copyright © 2007 Weldon Owen Inc.
and Williams-Sonoma Inc.

First printed in 2007.
10 9 8 7 6 5 4 3 2 1

ISBN-10: 0-8487-3168-9
ISBN-13: 978-0-8487-3168-7

Printed in China by SNP Leefung Printers Ltd.

CREDITS
Authors: Georgeanne Brennan: Pages 23, 34, 64, 78, 89, 120, 137, 166, 197; Heidi Haughty Cusick; Pages 110, 117, 135, 139-143, 156-159, 162, 175-176, 180, 189, 271; Lane Crowther: Pages 29, 37, 123, 133, 145, 190, 276; Janet Fletcher: Pages 59, 72-77, 82-87, 90-93, 96, 103-104, 107-109, 113, 131, 136, 154, 173, 185, 193, 248; Joyce Goldstein: Pages 81, 121, 152, 169–178, 208–211, 219, 258; Pamela Sheldon Johns: Pages 20, 26, 60-63, 99, 106, 114, 124-125, 160, 229; Joyce Jue: Pages 16, 38, 48, 55-56, 81, 126, 150-153, 165, 170, 184, 186, 273; Susan Manlin Katzman: Pages 225, 241; Kristine Kidd: Page 272; Betty Rosbottom: Pages 33, 40, 95, 100, 146, 169, 209, 218, 234, 251; Janeen Sarlin: Pages 30, 44, 202-206, 210-217, 220-222, 226, 230-233, 238-240, 243-247, 252, 267; Phillip Stephen Schultz: Page 183; Marie Simmons: Pages 43, 191; Joanne Weir: Pages 19, 22, 25, 28, 39, 51-52, 67-68, 194, 198

Photographers: Jeff Tucker and Kevin Hossler (cover), Richard Eskite (Introduction and recipe photography), Joyce Ouderk Pool (recipe photography for pages 63, 67, 127, 141, 159, 194, 203) and Allan Rosenberg (recipe photography for pages 11 (Mixed Berry Shortcakes), 13 (Lemon Almond Butter Cake), 252, 275, 279-284).

ACKNOWLEDGMENTS
Weldon Owen would like to thank Kevin Crafts, Lesli Neilson, and Kate Washington for all their expertise and hard work.